Roderick E. Lewis

The Corporate Recruitment Game

What Recruiters Don't Tell, And What Employers Try To Sell

Copyright

© 2012 by Roderick E. Lewis

All rights reserved. No part of this document may be reproduced or transmitted in any form or by any means, electronic, mechanical, photocopying, recording, or otherwise, without prior written permission of Roderick E. Lewis.

Dedication

"To enjoy good health, to bring true happiness to one's family, to bring peace to all, one must first discipline and control one's own mind. If a man can control his mind he can find the way to Enlightenment, and all wisdom and virtue will naturally come to him." – Buddha

This book is dedicated to all the job seekers who desire for companies to treat them like humans, not bits of uploaded data. Stay true to yourselves and continue to refine your personal brand. Look for the companies that value and respect people above all else. And most importantly, surround yourself with great friends who will constantly challenge you to do your best.

I would like to give special thanks to my parents (Louise Boyd Lewis and Robert Earl Lewis, Sr.), my aunt (Delores R. Boyd), and my close friends (Gabriel D. McCray and Carmen S. Jones) for their tireless dedication on making the writing of this book possible. This was a monumental task and would not have been completed without their support.

Preface

"Life is the art of being well deceived; and in order that the deception may succeed it must be habitual and uninterrupted." – William Hazlitt

I wrote the "The Corporate Recruitment Game" to inspire, educate, and enlighten the many job seekers all over the world who have been left dazed and confused by misrepresented employers, elaborate recruitment processes, shortsighted recruiters, and powerless Hiring Managers. The entire process companies use to entice job seekers to apply online is a game: and job seekers have to either play along with it, or create their own. There are many books written on how to get a corporate job, but they usually focus on playing the game laid out by large, multinational companies. They never seem to go into detail about why the flawed design of the corporate recruitment process is a joke that will not leave you laughing. I have personally spent almost 20 years as a job seeker dating back to my days as a college student. In those days, the job search process was relatively simple: you applied to the companies that visited your college's career center, or to the ones you met at career fairs and professional conferences. The World Wide Web as we know it today was in its nascent form, and online job postings were a novelty. Oh, how times have changed! Today, job postings are almost exclusively listed online, and companies have developed elaborate recruitment processes to handle the flood of applications they receive. On top of this, global companies are all jockeying for position to be the employer of choice for the best college graduates and experienced professionals. They are now using more marketing strategies and techniques to brand themselves as the employers for whom you want to work: however, don't expect the advertising campaigns they use to come with warning labels.

During my time as a job seeker, I have learned a few tips and tricks that I want to share with the next generation of job seekers. I am *"paying it forward"* by helping others to benefit from the knowledge it took me years to accumulate. I had always wanted to write a book, but did not know how to begin, or what topic to choose. Then I realized that it is best to write about what you know, and what you are passionate about. That combination led me to start writing the first pages in May 2011. I was inspired by all the world events from the Arab Spring to the Occupy Wall Street movement. Underscoring these movements was the desire for young people to have access to gainful employment opportunities. It was then that I realized that my passion for driving change in the corporate recruitment process, and my knowledge of how it works, was perfect for the times. I argue that it isn't the lack of jobs that is so frustrating, but rather, the lack of alternative recruitment methods and flexible hiring practices offered by global corporations. This leaves many talented job seekers with few opportunities to show how they could add value to a company unless they become experts in "writing job applications" and "gaming corporate interviews."

This book is for job seekers who want to know how the corporate recruitment game is played, and what they need to do in order to win. To win is to get hired, but the current recruitment game is not designed for the masses to win – regardless of what you've been told. If it were designed for you to win, then every job seeker who applied online would get offered a job. While writing this book I received several unsolicited job offers that would have been great opportunities for my career. It was ironic that these offers came just as I was in the middle of some of my most riveting chapters regarding the corporate recruitment game. I was afraid that I would not be able to complete this book if I had accepted any of those jobs. As fate would have it, circumstances intervened that allowed me to forego those opportunities in order to continue writing. Another "scare" occurred with the complete crashing of the computer which contained all my book drafts, as well as other irreplaceable information. I truly felt the world had come to an end that July morning. Without a minute to lose, I rushed to the nearest electronics store, and purchased a new laptop along with a file transfer cable. Thankfully, my old computer had just enough life in it to allow me to complete the transfer of all my files before it died completely.

Through my myriad job search campaigns and diverse work experiences, I have learned all about the unwritten rules of the corporate recruitment game: through trial and error, investigative research, and strategic networking. Once you learn the unwritten rules, you will be in a better position to overcome the whammies in the game. How so? Because you quickly understand that the best way to beat the corporate recruitment game, is to not play it at all. The dirty little secret in the corporate recruitment game is that there is more than one way to get added to the payrolls of your target companies. However, it is not easy: which is why only a small percentage of job seekers actually take the alternative routes outside of the well-traveled road of the online application. Most job seekers are woeful addicts of applying online, and in desperate need of rehab. While the *Betty Ford Clinic* isn't necessarily the best place to cure your ills, seeking the professional support of a competent career consultant is an important first step. With some *smart* work and dedication, you too, can change your ways, and venture onto a more rewarding job search track. Think of this book as the shock therapy that will get you on the road to recovery – the road to getting hired.

Table of Contents

Introduction

Level 1: Job Seekers Do The Playing
Chapter 1: Definition Of The Corporate Recruitment Game
Chapter 2: Corporate Employee Versus Professional Entrepreneur
Chapter 3: Corporate Recruiters Versus Talent Prevention Agents
Chapter 4: Hiring Managers: The Ugly, The Bad, And The Good
Chapter 5: Online Application Versus Private Investigation
Chapter 6: Game Play: Cheat Codes, Hints, And Tips
Chapter 7: Confessions Of A Corporate Recruiter

Level 2: Corporate Recruiters Do The Recruiting
Chapter 8: The Traditional Job Search
Chapter 9: Corporate Career Sites: Bait And Switch Advertising
Chapter 10: Job Postings: Confusion, Misdirection, And Disorder
Chapter 11: Applicant Tracking Systems: Anti-Talent Systems In Disguise
Chapter 12: Psychometric Testing: Quantifying The Standard Corporate Employee
Chapter 13: Interviews: Interrogations Versus Discussions
Chapter 14: Assessment Centers: The Rejection Centers
Chapter 15: Employment Offers: Low Cost Versus High Value
Chapter 16: Summary: Don't Waste Time Applying Online

Level 3: Hiring Managers Do The Hiring
Chapter 17: The Targeted Job Search
Chapter 18: Me Inc. Versus Me Too!
Chapter 19: Professional Service Provider Versus Average Corporate Employee
Chapter 20: Net-working Versus Not-working
Chapter 21: Marketing Portfolios Versus Traditional Résumés
Chapter 22: Personal Endorsements Versus Passive Referrals
Chapter 23: Pitching For Projects Versus Interviewing For Jobs
Chapter 24: Negotiated Compensation Versus Standard Compensation
Chapter 25: Summary: Journey To The Hiring Manager

Level 4: Global Companies Do The Deceiving
Chapter 26: Globally Ranked Companies
Chapter 27: Judging An Employer By Its Cover
Chapter 28: Job Posting Advertisements
Chapter 29: Career Site Communications
Chapter 30: Selection And Hiring
Chapter 31: Employer Ranking Publications
Chapter 32: Employee Engagement Reports
Chapter 33: Work-Life Benefits
Chapter 34: Volunteering And Social Investments
Chapter 35: Career Mobility And Development
Chapter 36: Diversity And Inclusion
Chapter 37: Web 2.0 Technologies
Chapter 38: Recognition And Compensation
Chapter 39: Workforce Sustainability Policies
Chapter 40: Summary: Assessing The Employer Value Proposition

Conclusion
The Job Seekers' Fables
Outro
About The Author

Introduction

"You have to learn the rules of the game. And then you have to play better than anyone else." – Albert Einstein

It is not easy for today's job seekers: social unrest, crippling debt, and mass layoffs. Whether you are a current student, recent graduate, or restless professional, you'll find that the burden of your job search is borne by you, and you alone. Don't expect any favors or tips from the companies for whom you want to work – especially the "so-called" great places to work. Their objective is to survive and prosper in an increasingly competitive global market that has nothing to do with your desire to get a job. You bear the burden of trying to figure out what's fact versus fiction as you begin your quest towards getting hired. Standing in the path of truth and transparency will be a plethora of vague job postings, ubiquitous job boards, flashy career sites, gatekeeping recruiters, and propaganda-wielding employer brands – oh my! It's enough to strike a sliver of fear in even the most intrepid job seekers. Getting extended an employment offer these days is not for the faint of heart. You need a sound strategy, executable tactics, and an ability to avoid job search tar pits in order to get the ultimate prize – an employment offer.

It's all a game – a shell game. But not like any shell game you have ever seen. In this game, you do not know the rules, and there is no user's manual. Yet, you'll be expected to play along until the music stops and you're the one who is left without a chair to sit on. **Welcome to the corporate recruitment game: where lies are disguised as half-baked truths, obfuscation is the norm, and transparency is the exception.** It's a wonderful game indeed – for the employers that play it, of course. Why? Because they get to cherry pick the "best applicants" from the daily harvest of online job applications while maintaining their positions as employers of choice. And for all those hundreds of thousands of job seekers who don't get selected for an interview – let alone the courtesy of an email rejection – they will be left scratching their heads wondering if it was even worth their time (and effort) to apply. But no one ever said you had to play the same game as everyone else – you just need to "play" better than everyone else.

"Kraft's staffing managers will only contact you if you are selected for an interview, and generally, this would occur within three weeks." – Kraft Foods Company

What is the point of the formal recruitment process? Is it: 1) to get an interview; or 2) to get a job? Most job seekers are so busy trying to get an interview that they forget the real objective is to get a job. The two objectives are completely different and will affect the way you plan your job search. When viewing the recruitment process as a journey to get an interview, you're basically setting yourself up with the nebulous goal of trying to appease the pleasures of a corporate recruiter. You are trying to create the perfect application that will pass through multiple recruitment process checkpoints before it meets (if you're lucky!) the actual eyes of a corporate recruiter. And it will more than likely be an incompetent recruiter at that! In the formal recruitment process, all roads lead to a recruiter. Wise job seekers follow the maxim: "Recruiters are to be avoided, not engaged." Why would you invest so much time in an online application just to get a "screening" interview with a recruiter whose business acumen is suspect at best, and non-existent at worst?

On the other hand, if you approach the recruitment process as a journey to get hired, then you are trying to get a job – not an interview. Therefore, you will eschew the formal recruitment process that is administered by corporate recruiters, and create a personalized recruitment process that is tailored to your specific objectives. All of your hard work and effort are now put into getting an audience with a Hiring Manager – not to interview, but to get a job. The interview process itself, whether given by a recruiter or Hiring Manager, is inherently a screening tool that favors the interviewer. You should never allow yourself to be interviewed in the traditional sense because it instantly positions the recruiter as the "lead" and you as the "follow" in the recruitment tango. Think about it, the interviewer is assuming the role of the "selector" while you assume the role of a job beggar – or more appropriately, someone who needs a job more than the company needs an employee. How does this give you any advantages, or position you as a resource person to be desired by the company? It doesn't. Therefore, a focus on getting hired means that you find ways to present your employee value proposition to the benefit of business-minded decision makers at your target employers.

Make no mistake about it, there are only two choices you can make when conducting your job search campaign: 1) apply online to be screened by a recruiter; or 2) speak directly to a Hiring Manager. Option one is loaded with the trap doors and fake mirrors that form the heart of the corporate recruitment game. Option two is the road rarely taken that bypasses the game. Many job seekers are inevitably drawn to option one because they are unable to **break the "psychological rules" of the corporate recruitment process** which imply that the only path to become an employee is through the bosom of the recruiter – the online application. It is standard corporate recruitment practice to lull job seekers into believing there is only one path to getting hired. This belief is nurtured by the explosion in online job boards and corporate career sites. Recruiters are all too happy to send you directly to the online application because it makes their lives easier. But why should you be trying to make their lives easier? Why would you want to do your song and dance for them? You're not planning to work for them, and you most certainly don't need to rely on them to screen you out (or filter you in). The only person you should want reviewing your credentials for a job is the Hiring Manager, or someone with direct functional experience from the department in which you desire to work.

Which do you prefer: a corporate recruitment process, or a talent acquisition process? That's a trick question! They are the same – therefore, you should not prefer either one. They are both processes designed to produce a standardized product according to predefined specifications. For example, in manufacturing processes, the goal is to eliminate any defective parts so as to improve the yield of finished products that meet a predefined standard. At each stage along the manufacturing process there are inspectors and quality control agents whose job it is to assess every nook and cranny of the component parts, as well as the finished product. It is all designed for mass production and duplication of the specified products. The corporate recruitment process isn't too different. Job seekers become the raw materials fed into a hungry machine that spits them out, and stamps them like barcoded drones to be scanned, sorted, and selected according to specifications. Hiring Managers specify the candidate criteria, and their henchmen (corporate recruiters) manage the stages of the process that screen out the "bad" and "defective" applicants, while ushering in the ideal ones. So when you apply online, you'll only pass through if you meet the standards that recruiters will be assessing. If you fall short at any point in the process, it's game over. If you come out the other side of the recruitment process funnel, then it is because you are as close to the ideal finished product as per the Hiring Manager's specifications.

"When we receive your application, the recruitment team will review it initially to ensure that you have answered all the questions and met our minimum requirements in terms of education etc. Your application will then be passed to one of our professional development managers for full review." – IBM

For each job you apply to there can only be one winner – the person who gets hired. You can be assured that the corporate recruitment game attracts a lot of players; therefore, it won't be an easy task to emerge as the winner. If your objective in the game is to get hired, then applying through an online recruitment process is the wrong play. Nowhere on a company's website or job postings will it say that you'll be hired for a job by applying online. They merely tell you that you have to apply online in order to be considered for a job – huge difference. The words are very important. When you don't properly define the words of the corporate recruitment game, you'll always be left more confused and prone to choose poor job search tactics. Everyone who applies online to their target companies will not get hired. Therefore, the job seekers who apply are merely being recruited to enter a process – not to be hired. **If online applications are just for the pleasure of being considered, then there are better uses for your time if your objective is to be hired.** Your time can be spent trying to play the game, or trying to beat the game. In most professional sports, there are two methods to win games: 1) you can outplay your opponent through superior strategy and execution; or 2) you can outplay the system that controls the rules of the game.

"Upon successfully completing the CV evaluation stage, you'll receive an information pack containing more details about ING as well as some useful tips to improve your chance of success in the rest of the selection procedure. After all, if you've got potential, we want to see it!" – Ing Direct

Many job seekers attempt to outplay the corporate recruitment game, and end up getting discarded like waste from a trash bin. Trying to beat the game is like a professional athlete trying to trick the referees (rules officials) into making favorable calls that penalize the opposing team's players. This happens in soccer when players fake an injury, or in basketball when players feign a foul. Since job seekers don't know who else is applying for the same jobs, they find it more practical to attempt to outplay the game by writing the "best applications" and giving the "best interviews". This is great for the recruiters managing the process because as long as you're concentrating on trying to beat the game, it means you're not concentrating on trying to be hired! That leaves them in complete control over who gets selected and who gets rejected. Remember, you do not have to play the corporate recruitment game, but you do need to play better than everyone else.

Why is it that so many job seekers are scrambling to work for companies that they know little about other than the companies' name brand recognition and product brands? Well, that probably has more to do with a company's employer branding (EB) campaigns than with their actual understanding of the company's employer value proposition (EVP). Think of EB as an advertising campaign, and EVP as a product (or service). Companies use EB to promote their EVP in order to convince you to apply to their jobs and promote them as best places to work. When you find yourself unwittingly drawn to work for a company because of its heft in the market, then you've been captivated by the employer branding hocus pocus (EBHP). What is EBHP? It is the dark side of employer branding that is equivalent to false advertising. It is all of the seedy, underhanded, and duplicitous efforts used by employers to sell you on the sizzle, but deliver you an undercooked steak. EBHP is developed by Human Resources (HR) departments in conjunction with savvy Marketing departments to paint a picture of the ideal employer that you crave in your mind's eye. It will encourage you to apply online to job after job at the same company even after having been rejected multiple times.

"Reaching qualified, talented individuals is a task in and of itself, but when trying to attract college students for internships or entry level positions, your recruitment marketing strategy must leverage new technology to reach students where they're at – and it's not just on campus. By using new and exciting tools to engage talented students and build their employment brand, Ernst & Young can ensure entry-level talent will look to them as a top choice upon graduation." – www.talentminded.com

What EBHP does not tell you is that only a few of the thousands of job seekers will be contacted from online applications, and even fewer will actually get hired. Nor does it communicate the pitfalls of becoming a corporate employee, and being subjected to constant job insecurity. Do not feel bad if you have been a victim of EBHP: it happens to the majority of job seekers. You are as susceptible to EBHP as a five-year old child is to a McDonald's Happy Meal. The real tragedy, however, is that you do not understand the implications that EBHP has on your job search. It lulls you into a false sense of security where you feel the world is a fair place for job seekers, and that companies are obliged to provide you with the best workplace environment to suit your specific talents. In your quest to become an employee, you are blinded from seeing the true nature of today's corporations all over the world: they are in business to make money – not provide jobs.

When you embrace how employers operate the corporate recruitment game, you will be better prepared to take on the challenges and bypass the traps that will litter the path along your job search – assuming you decide to play the game. Have you ever paused to ask yourself why you apply online? It is an important question to answer before you decide whether or not to play the corporate recruitment game. Though there are numerous reasons why job seekers apply online, the top three that I have found to be the most common are: 1) they believe that it is the only way to get hired; 2) recruiters and misguided colleagues tell them to do so; and 3) every job posting on career sites, job boards, and social media sites tells them to do so. This misinformation leads many job seekers to be hoodwinked, hornswoggled, bamboozled, swindled, conned, and led astray. They believe that applying online will get them one step closer to becoming a corporate employee. For some it will, but for many others it won't – at least not in the corporate jobs they desire. Regardless, the corporate recruitment game would have every job seeker believe that applying online is the only way to get hired, and it will use EBHP to reinforce this belief.

"Since recruiters are on the front line in the battle to attract candidates from a continually shrinking pool of top talent, it's more important than ever before to aggressively market the benefits of working for the client company. Recruiters must sell the value proposition of working for the company by regaling prospects with enticing emotionally laden tales of the company story. And recruiters should harness the power of social recruiting to spread the good word about a client company." – www.recruiter.com

EBHP will espouse the lore of the corporation to the best and worst job seekers alike. The above quote is an example of EBHP and it is no different than the hundreds of advertising messages you are bombarded with each and every day from companies hawking their products. EBHP is like a virus that makes you throw all rationale out the window. You will believe what you read on a company's website and its job postings. You will believe that a corporate recruiter's mission is to find a job for you that best suits your skill set. You will believe the HR department is an employee advocate that seeks to maximize your ability to do your job by creating the optimal workplace environment. You will believe the employer rankings publications that classify your target employers as great places to work. You will believe that your job is secure as long as you perform above average, and get along with your co-workers. Indeed, you will believe in all the corporate fairytales, folktales, and fables. **If you believe that you are suffering from any of these EBHP symptoms, seek immediate attention from a competent career consultant.**

Part One

Job Seekers Do The Playing

Chapter 1
Definition Of The Corporate Recruitment Game

"I am very much afraid of definitions, and yet one is almost forced to make them. One must take care, too, not to be inhibited by them." – Robert Delaunay

There are not many formal definitions of the **"Corporate Recruitment Game"**. In fact, you will not find any hard evidence that it even exists: this is why the game continues to be played at the highest level. **What is the corporate recruitment game?** It is a company's two-part strategy to bait job seekers with employer branding campaigns, and then hook them with online applications. The characters in the game are the job seekers, corporate recruiters, and Hiring Managers. They each use their own bag of tricks, spells, and potions to achieve their objectives – which usually are contradictory. The game pits everyone against each other by fostering competition rather than collaboration. It's a chess game where job seekers are the "Pawns", corporate recruiters are the "Queens ", and Hiring Managers are the "Kings". Job seekers have to sharpen their swords and do battle with a phalanx of corporate recruiters in order to reach the Hiring Managers. This battle ensures that the overall objective of the corporate recruitment game stays intact: keep the top job seekers applying online fighting to become employees, instead of becoming entrepreneurs – or being hired by the competition.

Companies justify the tactics of the corporate recruitment game as their best chance to win "The War for Talent", which for all intents and purposes, is a manufactured war. It signals the end of the corporation's role as a place to train and develop the average college graduate, and the beginning of "best and the brightest" hiring mantras. Major corporations develop elaborate recruitment schemes and send out hoards of corporate henchmen to battle over a supposedly finite talent pool of university graduates and experienced professionals. It's a king's war waged by wealthy crown companies that realize the high stakes of hiring the star employees whose intellectual capital will generate a disproportionate share of wealth in the corporate coffers. Corporations are not interested in the scores of college graduates hitting the job market each year: they are only interested in the identifiable top candidates. No company can expect to remain in business by hiring the lowest-performing graduates and professionals. Corporations have long realized that universities don't graduate scores of top students: they merely attract scores of students who graduate. The vast majority of college graduates will be degree holders who offer no substantive value to a company – yet they will expect the same salary and benefits as the top candidates. Separating the wheat from the chaff among job seeking college graduates is a chief function of the corporate recruitment game.

"Google is reportedly handing out as much as $100 million to keep its employees from fleeing. Too many smart Google execs have hit the exits lately, and the company wants to keep the big brains in house. Google isn't trying to keep employees to make itself better, it's to prevent its rivals from weakening Google." – www.businessinsider.com

Global corporations don't want smart people starting the next Amazon, Apple, Facebook, or Google that will disrupt their business – or put them out of business altogether. The 2001 movie, *Antitrust*, loosely illustrates this point – albeit to an extreme level. By design, the corporate recruitment game significantly influences the majority of the best and the brightest job seekers to continue taking the conventional path to paid employment. That is a major reason why companies invest in employer branding activities, and encourage job seekers to apply online *en masse*. Their goal is not to entertain the swarm of applicants hoping to strike gold: it is only to find the few gold nuggets hidden within the swarm. When your objective is to become a corporate employee, you first need to understand how companies go about selecting applicants; and more importantly, how they reject them. You will need to learn the rules of the game, and how to play it without playing it. The corporate recruitment game is meant to ensure the survival of the global corporation. It is a Darwinian game rewarding the corporations that play the best by giving them access to tier-1 job seeker talent. The corporations that get left behind have to contend for tier-2 and tier-3 talent.

"Having too many "second-class" (or even "third-class") citizens in your business will not do a great deal for productivity, or the quality of the services you are trying to provide." – www.theglobeandmail.com

Many job seekers have no clue that the recruitment process is part of a larger game that has nothing to do with creating jobs. They are too enthralled with the prospect of becoming corporate employees to see how they are being used as pawns in someone else's game. The corporate recruitment game assigns little value to the job seekers who will make up the corps of average corporate employees: those of whom can be eliminated at any time when economic conditions dictate, or when the CEO needs to pad the quarterly results. More importantly, **the corporate recruitment game serves a higher purpose: it is the means to keep the company from meeting an untimely end.** CEO's and major shareholders understand the risks to their profits if they are unable to attract, select, and hire the cream of the crop. The game has only intensified over the past few decades as the competition for talented individuals has been globalized. Corporations have always played "war games" to stay ahead of their competition, and to survive in an increasingly hostile market. The original corporate game started out as the suppression of disruptive technologies in order for companies to extend monopolies and barriers to entry. Then it moved to the outright purchase of disruptive technologies and start-ups in order to limit competition. And now, in its latest iteration, it has moved to the suppression and purchase of disruptive talent: better to "hoard and hire" the top job seekers than to compete against them.

"Intel's Accelerated Leadership Program (ALP) is a unique post-MBA rotational leadership program. Intel's executive team designed the ALP to transform passionate and ambitious MBA graduates into Intel's most influential future leaders. From day one, ALP associates have the opportunity to drive our core businesses and help lead Intel into new multibillion-dollar growth segments, such as consumer electronics, smart phones, and PCs for emerging markets." –Intel

"The search for the best and the brightest will become a constant, costly battle, a fight with no final victory. Not only will companies have to devise more imaginative hiring practices; they will also have to work harder to keep their best people. In the new economy, competition is global, capital is abundant, ideas are developed quickly and cheaply, and people are willing to change jobs often." – www.fastcompany.com

The Game Pieces

To understand how the corporate recruitment game is played, you will need to learn the definitions of the game pieces, processes, and people. The game starts with employer branding, and ends with the Hiring Manager. What happens in between is shrouded in mystery, and wrapped in riddles. Few people understand exactly what is **"Employer Branding"** and its role in the corporate recruitment game. It is the oil that lubricates the mighty engine of the corporate recruitment process. It is no different than product branding that serves to sell you on an "employment experience" that may or may not exist: and in all likelihood, one that you will probably not be hired to personally know.

1. **Employer Branding.** It is the marketing and advertising a company undertakes to position itself as an ideal employer in the eyes of job seekers, current employees, and any other employment stakeholders. More importantly, it is used as the main promotional campaign to entice the best job seekers to apply online. Every major company uses some form of employer branding: its "signal strength" and impact on target audiences will be dependent on the resources allocated by the company.

2. **Employer Brand.** The measure of an employer's features and benefits as measured by the feelings, attitudes, opinions, and sentiments of job seekers and current employees. This also includes the company's reputation as an employer of choice. Every company has an employer brand: some are positive, some are negative, and some are nebulous. The term "Employer Value Proposition" (EVP) is also used.

The **"Corporate Recruitment Process"** is an important term to define as it is the engine that powers the entire corporate recruitment game. Throughout this book, I will use the terms "corporate recruitment process", "formal recruitment process", and "recruitment process" interchangeably. A company's recruitment process is designed for one purpose: to find the standard corporate employees who will keep the corporate titanic afloat.

1. **Corporate Recruitment Process.** Refers to the formal process of attracting, screening, and selecting qualified people for a job. The process begins when you complete an online application and ends when you are either rejected or hired. The terms "Application Process", "Hiring Process", and "Selection Process" are also used.

2. **Talent Acquisition Process.** This is just a fancier name for the recruitment process that became the buzz *du jour* in the first decade of the 21st century. It's the equivalent of putting lipstick on a pig. The term "Talent Selection Process" is also used.

3. **Applicant Tracking System.** This is the software program that facilitates job posting searches, online job applications, applicant status in the recruitment process, and the storing of applicant details in a searchable database. It allows recruiters to automate the applicant screening process, and generate the dreaded rejection emails that have become the staple of online application lore. The system is currently being rebranded under *les noms de jour* of "Talent Network", "Talent Community", and "Recruiting CRM".

The current recruitment processes used by global companies tend to treat most job seekers as "job beggars" rather than "resource people". What's the difference? A job beggar is someone who's desperate for a job – any job! It isn't clear what value job beggars will bring to a company. On the other hand, resource persons are sought after by companies for their recognized value and ability to positively affect business metrics. Certainly, your intent isn't to be defined as a job beggar! The most common formal terms used in the recruitment lexicon to define the **"Potential Employees"** from the scores of job seekers are:

1. **Job Applicants.** This term is reserved for individuals who have completed online applications and are currently awaiting a decision on their candidacy.

2. **Job Candidates.** Usually this term is reserved for individuals whose online applications meet the standards set in the applicant tracking systems, thus allowing them to advance in the recruitment process.

3. **Prospective Candidates.** Any job seeking individual who visits a company's website, or sees a job posting advertisement online (or print) falls under this category. The term "potential applicants" is also used.

4. **Active Candidates.** Individuals that are actively seeking new employment opportunities. These candidates can be currently employed or unemployed.

5. **Passive Candidates.** Someone who is not looking for a job, but would be open to taking one if the right opportunity came along. Many recruiters believe these candidates are more valuable simply because they are "not" actively seeking to leave their current employers.

6. **Job Seekers Who Follow The Rules.** They are individuals who single-mindedly follow the rules of the corporate recruitment process per companies' instructions and apply online; or through whatever channel the company has requested. They generally follow the "apply and wait" model which converts them into passive participants in the company's recruitment process. A rejection at any point in this process means the end of their job candidacy.

7. **Job Seekers Who Break The Rules.** They are individuals who use multiple channels to bypass the corporate recruitment process. They generally follow the "network and create" model which allows them to facilitate their own self-designed (and self-managed) recruitment process with target companies. A rejection in one channel does not automatically end their job candidacy.

Though there are various levels and types of employees found in global companies, the only type that will be referred to in this book are the **"Corporate Employees"**. They are the individuals who work in professional roles requiring university degrees – excluding CEO's and high-level Executives. Throughout this book, I will use the terms "corporate employees" and "employees" interchangeably. There are essentially two types of corporate employees coveted by global corporations:

1. **Corporate Drones.** It may sound like a derogatory term, but it is what the average corporate employee will become: a mindless, spineless worker that operates without individual thought, or spontaneous action. They are oftentimes brainwashed into believing that *people are the company's most important asset*. Usually corporate drones are not hired – they are made: a result of a company's own bureaucracy and people management practices. They are often classified as costs to be controlled and contained. They are the corporate soldiers who dutifully carry out their orders. Their careers will be defined by promotions in place, and arrested development. The term "Worker Bees" is also used.

2. **Corporate Promotables.** Only a selected few will ever achieve this status. They are usually brainwashed with an air of superiority in order to feel special. They will be the managers and leaders responsible for ensuring a company's success primarily through cutting costs and increasing assets. They are identified early in their employment tenures (oftentimes before they are even hired) and given access to corporate

executives, placed on high-value projects, and prepared for international assignments. They are likely to be placed into specially-designed leadership programs that give them broad exposure to global business operations. They are the main target that the corporate recruitment game was designed to capture. The term "High-Potentials" is also used.

The key players that promulgate the tenets of the corporate recruitment game are the **"Corporate Recruiters"**. These are the Human Resources employees whose job it is to manage all (or part) of the operations and administration of the recruitment process: job advertising, candidate sourcing, and employee on-boarding. They make the rules of their company's recruitment process and are indeed the dreaded Gatekeepers. In this book, I will only focus on the role of the in-house corporate recruiters whose sole purpose is to staff their organizations with professional employees in business and technical roles. All corporate recruiters don't simply fall into one category, as many job seekers falsely believe. Though recruiters can have functional backgrounds that include engineering, finance, marketing, and operations; the vast majority of corporate recruiters will only have functional experience (and education) in human resources fields. Throughout this book, I will use the terms "corporate recruiter" and "recruiter" interchangeably. Nowadays, the terms have given way to fancier names meant to give the role more clout, such as:

1. **Talent Acquisition Specialist.** The recruiter focused mainly on the administrative and operational duties of the recruitment process, marketplace trends, and competitor practices. The term "Talent Acquisition Consultant" is also used.

2. **Talent Acquisition Manager.** The recruiter focused on short and long term hiring plans that support the business across a number of metrics. The term "Talent Manager" is also used.

3. **College Recruitment(Relations) Manager.** The recruiter focused mainly on student and graduate recruitment

operations among other campus brand building initiatives. The terms "University Relations Manager" and "Graduate Recruitment Manager" are also used.

4. **Employer Brand(ing) Manager.** The recruiter focused on general recruitment of students and professionals, but with the main responsibility for internal and external employer of choice marketing initiatives. This recruiter will focus more on the marketing and advertising strategies needed to attract the top job seekers to apply online. The term "Employer Brand(ing) Consultant" is also used.

Finally, the definition for the people who ultimately decide who gets hired: the **"Hiring Managers"**. They are the decision makers or other high-level business managers who have the final say over the recruitment process end game. They can be parsed into two types:

1. **Direct Decision Maker.** This is the person whom the job seeker would report to upon a successful hire. They will assess the job candidates presented to them by recruiters, as well as those reaching their offices through other channels.

2. **Indirect Decision Maker.** This is the person who is either over the Hiring Manager, or is an influential stakeholder in the hiring decision. They oftentimes operate through shrewd politics rather than brute force, and also serve as sounding boards for the direct decision makers.

With all of these terms being thrown around, it's no accident that job seekers continue to fight a losing battle by applying online. Most of the terms are meant to confuse and disorient you by tricking you into chasing the wrong rabbit. Terms such as "Talent Acquisition Manager" and "Talent Acquisition Process" illustrate this practice. Who wouldn't want to speak to a Talent Acquisition Manager or enter into a Talent Acquisition Process? Every job seeker who applies to a job will want to believe deep down that someone considers them a talented person. But the reality is that companies do not consider every job seeker as a talent any more than they consider every employee as a talent. These terms do more to prey on your ego than to appeal to your reason. They goad you into applying online because the alternative would be for you to consider yourself a "non-talent" – and who wants to be that? Keep in mind, however, that "talent is in the eye of the beholder": with the beholders being the corporate recruiters and Hiring Managers.

These are just examples of the power of the employer branding hocus pocus I detailed in the introduction. Ponzi scheme marketing to make you think that recruiters are more powerful than they actually are, and that the recruitment process is more effective than it actually is. Boiler room tactics to convince you that applying online is the best investment of your time, only to dump you like a penny stock later. Cheap parlor tricks to persuade entrepreneurial-minded job seekers that being a corporate employee is the safest bet, while simultaneously announcing massive layoffs for unsuspecting employees. EBHP will spin fairytale stories to mystify the best companies for leaders, high-potential employees, and unmatched compensation. You bear the burden of identifying fact from fiction, reality from fantasy, and hearsay from testimony. Understanding the form and function of the chess pieces involved in the corporate recruitment game will help you develop a game plan to beat it – or avoid it entirely. You have to know how the game is played against you in order to appreciate the strategy of not playing it at all. **The game is filled with barriers designed to outmaneuver, outwit, and outflank the average job seeker: all to keep them from speaking to the most important player on the chess board – the Hiring Manager.**

Chapter 2
Corporate Employees Versus Professional Entrepreneurs

"An entrepreneur assumes the risk and is dedicated and committed to the success of whatever he or she undertakes." – Victor Kiam

Before you jump head first into the treacherous waters of the corporate recruitment game, you need to make a defining choice: be a corporate employee, or be a professional entrepreneur. The vast majority of job seekers only desire to work for someone else and usually do not think of themselves as entrepreneurs. However, there is a growing minority of job seekers who have the desire and the ability to become entrepreneurs: yet many of them falsely believe they first need to work for someone else in order to "gain" experience before venturing off on their own. **So the implication is that the path to entrepreneurship is paved with jagged rocks, while the path to being a corporate employee is paved with smooth pebbles.** Is there really any more inherent risk in becoming a professional entrepreneur versus becoming a corporate employee? If you desire to be a corporate employee because you are not yet clear on your professional direction then that may be the best objective for you. At least you'll earn a paycheck while you learn something of value to somebody – hopefully! Some corporate employees have great success and are well-compensated for their understanding of (and contribution to) the company.

Unfortunately for most job seekers, they will never see the upper echelons of the corporate pay scale, just like every amateur athlete will never become part of a professional team that would pay him millions of dollars. If it were so easy, then every corporate employee could look forward to ultra-high earnings and a comfortable lifestyle for themselves and their loved ones. Though it is easy for job seekers to assume that being a corporate employee is the least risky employment proposition, there are employees being fired in droves everyday – the vast majority having no safety net other than unemployment benefits. In the end, you will still be an employee who has no control over how long you remain employed, or what the conditions of that employment will be. Unless you are deemed a "corporate promotable" by the company elders, you will just be the average "corporate drone" stuck in the middle of the pay scale. With outsourcing now an ingrained business strategy, corporate employees always run the risk of having their entire department relocated, right-sized, or shut down entirely.

"Qantas has considered plans to outsource all its ground-handling operations during this decade as part of a longer-term strategy to reshape the airline and lower labour costs." – www.smh.com.au

Most employees have only one job and rarely have the time, energy, or ability to earn income from a side gig. The greatest risk to being a corporate employee is for the highly innovative and creative job seekers. Why? Because all of their intellectual property will be legally owned by the employer. This means if you create the next big thing, you'll still earn your same salary (and hopefully get a nice bonus) while the corporate executives and shareholders reap the millions of dollars your creation is worth. The late Jack Kirby, a former employee of Marvel Incorporated, found this out the hard way. Mr. Kirby created the comic book characters: Iron Man, X-Men, Thor, Incredible Hulk, and many others. He made billions of dollars for the company, but he did not have ownership rights for his own creations. If you have a defined career brand and have a strong reputation within your network, entrepreneurship is an option worth weighing. Even though most job seekers will seek their fortunes working for someone else (and some will do quite well), some may find that it is more lucrative to work for themselves.

"Google engineers are encouraged to take 20 percent of their time to work on something company-related that interests them personally. This means that if you have a great idea, you always have time to run with it." – www.nytimes.com

If you have the ability to innovate and create for someone else, then you can do it for yourself. If you have the ability to convince someone to hire you for a job that you create for yourself, then you can function independently as a professional entrepreneur. This gives you the option to control the rights and the financial arrangements of your intellectual property. You're able to have multiple sources of income and not rely on a sole company for your economic security. As an entrepreneur, you'll always have the means and the know-how to generate income for yourself independent of what is going on in the world marketplace. Where the majority of job seekers only assess the risks of working for themselves, the small minority of professional entrepreneurs also assess the rewards. Being an entrepreneur doesn't mean you have to create the next Google or Facebook. It simply means that you gain control over how you will be paid for your time, deliverables, and intellectual property. There will always be a risk that your business model will not be profitable, or that you will fail outright. However, there is also the risk that you will be fired as a corporate employee, or have your career path controlled by someone else who doesn't deem you worthy to move up the corporate ladder.

A professional entrepreneur will gain much more business experience and market intelligence than the average corporate employee. Some job seekers, no matter how smart and gifted, just don't fit the corporate mold and will never make it through a corporate recruitment process. For example, Bill Gates and Mark Zuckerberg are famous for their reputations as being socially awkward. If they had chosen to go through corporate recruitment processes, they probably would have landed backroom-programming jobs at best. They most certainly would not have been put into positions that would have fairly compensated them for their value. When you become a corporate employee it means that someone else controls what you do and to what degree you will do it. In contrast, becoming a professional entrepreneur gives you the freedom to control the depth of your business acumen to whatever degree you desire. There is no better way to stand out from the mass of me-too job seekers than by adding the professional entrepreneur title to your career brand. You might even be able to position yourself to lead a start-up project within an established company should you decide in the future to become a corporate employee: the possibilities are endless. However, only consider pursuing a professional entrepreneur track if you are able to do the following at a minimum:

1. **Create New Products Or Services.** Job seekers who have the ability to see niches and gaps in the marketplace can capitalize by creating products and services aligned with their career brand and expertise. Bill Gates and Mark Zuckerberg were still university students when they started their companies, thus being an entrepreneur is dependent on your ingenuity – not seniority. The internet and low cost technologies have leveled the playing field and have removed many of the financial risks for starting a business. Even if you spot an opportunity in an area unrelated to your expertise, it is still not out of reach: you always have the option to operate the business independently, or with partners.

2. **Create New Uses For Existing Products Or Services.** Job seekers can also innovate new ways to tackle business challenges that meet client and consumer needs with existing technologies. If you see how a particular application can be used beneficially in a way for which it was not originally designed, then you can capitalize on it. Michael Lazaridis, the founder of Research in Motion (maker of Blackberry phones), got the idea to start the company when someone at a trade show told him how Coca-Cola machines use wireless technology to signal that they need refilling. There are myriad services and business practices that can be redesigned using existing technologies. The limits are only with the imaginations of those capable of doing so.

Last Chance To Exit The Corporate Employee Bandwagon

Rarely will a company accurately value highly-talented job seekers for their intellectual property and above average skills. If you become a corporate employee, you will have no rights to your intellectual property that will be used to make the company money. On the flip side, the company can easily lose money by hiring employees who don't fit their workplace environment. These are the risks that are inherent in any employment arrangement for both employers and employees. Nevertheless, instead of holding yourself hostage by the possible risks to your employment security, you would be wise to become adept at risk management. That is what smart companies do! Many job seekers are set on priming themselves to be corporate employees and letting someone else assume the risk of business failure. What these job seekers don't take into consideration is the fact that the vast majority of skills they gain from one employer won't always allow them to command higher compensation or easily transition to future employers. How useful would it be to your career to work at a company that still relied on print advertising when the leading companies are investing in social media advertising? Most corporate employees will be limited to the job scope defined by their superiors, as well as the company's business policies and practices.

Being a professional entrepreneur allows you to control your own career development, adapt in real time to market changes, and pursue the opportunities most profitable to you. If you are unemployed and job searching, it's always easy to say that you can't afford to start your own business: but can you afford to remain unemployed? If you are employed and job searching, it's always easy to say that you can't afford to quit your job: but can you afford to be fired? If you decide that you want to be a professional entrepreneur then you can put this book down right now and go start your company! If that leap is too big to make, and the very idea fills you with dread from head to toe, then that is a sign that it is not meant for you at this time – if ever. However, since you have to do something to earn a living, it will be best for you to use your education and experience to work for someone else – namely, a large corporation. Otherwise, you will find it difficult to pay for a decent standard of living while simultaneously pursuing some manner of financial freedom. Keep in mind, however, that being a corporate employee does not equate to employment stability or security.

The Process To Become A Corporate Employee

It is advisable to think like a professional entrepreneur during your job search quest to become a corporate employee. **There are essentially two roads you can take to become a corporate employee: 1) use the traditional job search; or 2) use the targeted job search.** The corporate recruitment game is designed to take advantage of job seekers using the traditional job search because it is based on entering into recruitment processes controlled by corporate recruiters. Thus, the company is able to control who gets selected and hired, and who gets rejected from further consideration. In contrast, the targeted job search is a disruptive method that wreaks havoc on corporate recruitment processes because its users find alternative ways to become employees – thereby escaping the standard screening methodologies. It's a Trojan Horse strategy right out of the ancient Greek playbook that facilitates your entering a company while avoiding the detection of gatekeeping recruiters. The company wins the recruitment game only when it can condition job applicants through the formal recruitment process to ensure they match the standard corporate employee mold. You win the game if you can get extended an employment offer while avoiding being brainwashed with the corporate gobbledygook inherent in the formal recruitment process. Thereby you keep your mind free, remain unplugged from the game, and prevent infection from the EBHP virus.

The corporate recruitment game relies on the same level of control enjoyed by casino houses that decide who wins the jackpot. Yet, just like in the movie, *Ocean's Eleven*, there is always a player who knows how to beat the house. This is why companies prefer to screen all their potential employees for any known defects that would render them unsuitable to corporate brainwashing. Non-believers in corporate hegemony, those unable to surrender their will to authority, and independent thinkers need not apply. It isn't enough to merely hire the best and the brightest along with the appropriate role players, but also to make sure they are "corporate ready". In professional sports like the National Football League (NFL), talent scouts rate potential draft picks on whether or not they are "NFL ready": meaning they have demonstrated their aptitude by passing carefully-designed mental and physical exercises deemed necessary for success in the NFL. The corporate recruitment process serves a similar function in determining which job seekers will be deemed "corporate ready". Going through the recruitment process allows companies to gather all of your personal and professional statistics in order to predict your future success. It allows them to take you through a series of exercises where you will indeed feel like you are trying out for a roster spot on a professional sports team. Whether or not you make the team (get hired) is entirely up to how you fare against your competition.

"The next stage following first-round interviews will be an assessment centre. The aim of this centre is to give you a feel for what working at BP is like. For example, you'll be part of a small team given a business exercise that will ask you to deal with a series of challenges. During the day you'll also complete a mixture of tasks - some individual, some group-based - so that we can get as complete a picture of your strengths and abilities as possible." – BP

The corporate recruitment game uses the same framework as the NFL in how it segments its talent. Professional players are drafted by the NFL from the corps of college student athletes. Depending on their talent level, they will be labeled as one of the following: 1) role players; or 2) stars. Anyone who keeps up with professional sports knows that the success of a team depends upon the talent of its stars. Finding the next Aaron Rogers, Tom Brady, or Tim Tebow is the ultimate goal of any team recruiting players from the student athletes entering the annual NFL draft. And so it is with the corporate recruitment game where role players and stars will be carefully selected from the corps of graduates at top universities all over the world. It is a star-driven game where finding the next Mark Zuckerberg, Bill Gates, or Steve Jobs is the ultimate objective. While you won't be evaluated for how fast you run the 50-yard dash, you can expect to be hooked up to a virtual web of scanners that monitor your application writing ability, problem-solving speed, and interviewing skills – at a minimum. As with the NFL, the job seekers coming from recognized universities will get more visibility (and consideration) than those who don't.

Chapter 3
Corporate Recruiters: The Talent Prevention Agents

"After you submit your resume, you'll get an automated e-mail to let you know we received it. Our Human Resources department recruiters will review your materials. We get a lot of resumes, so you might not get a personal reply. Please continue to update your resume for future consideration." – 3M Corporation

As a job seeker, you may not fully understand the ins and outs of the corporate recruitment game, and the implications it will have on your quest to become an employee at your target companies. No matter how smart you (think) are or how many accomplishments you have, they are all meaningless unless you receive the blessing and the favor of the "One-Eyed Gatekeepers": the corporate recruiters. The selection and recruitment of employees in many large companies is held hostage by corporate recruiters – much to the chagrin of many job seekers. Why one group within any company should have so much power over the systems and mechanisms used to decide who gets to work is beyond explanation. With very few exceptions, recruiters act more as talent prevention agents than as talent acquisition agents. The whole mindset of the average corporate recruiter is to "screen out" job seekers who don't meet the requirements of stitched-together job postings that have the appearance of Mary Shelley's Frankenstein Monster.

Most recruiters are too busy (and too incompetent) to collaborate with Hiring Managers on writing job descriptions through the use of formal assessments to determine the required knowledge, skills, and abilities (ksa's) of the job. They expedite the process by using a "cut and paste" job posting that bears little semblance to what will actually be performed on the job. **It's far easier for these recruiters to make job seekers play a game of "Best Résumé Writer Wins" than to actually search for talented job seekers who can add value to their companies.** This behavior causes organizations to miss out on individuals who could be assets to other departments through existing job openings, or through jobs created to leverage their unique ksa's. Because of this bad behavior, many potential employees never get an opportunity to show how they can benefit their target companies. But why should your fortunes be tied to the whims of a recruiter? Furthermore, why should you be punished if your résumé doesn't win a beauty contest? If résumé aesthetics is a required skill, then it should be written in the job description before it is posted and advertised to the public! At least then you could decide if it is worth the investment to pay a professional résumé writer to give yours an "extreme makeover".

In talking with job seekers – both employed and unemployed – I realize that many are frustrated and angry at a number of things involving the lack of transparency in the formal recruitment process. More often than not, these cases are limited to the job seekers who spend the majority of their time applying to jobs online. The main themes I hear are:

- **Why didn't the company acknowledge receipt of my application materials?**
- **Why didn't the company respond quickly to tell me if I'll be interviewed or not?**
- **Why didn't the company contact me for an interview?**

All are very valid questions. And in a perfect world you would receive prompt replies to your job applications with a box of chocolates hand delivered to you the next day. But let's be clear on one thing: the recruitment process was not designed to build your self-esteem or quench your ego's thirst. It was designed by the company to hire the best (or most available) applicant. Of course, one could argue (and rightfully so), that a company's recruitment process should be designed to make sure that even rejected job applicants are treated with a modicum of dignity and respect. After all, they are not only potential consumers of the company's products (or services), but also potential brand advocates. However, recruitment processes are not managed by business-minded people who can see the value in leveraging the insights of the rejected (as well as selected) applicants by treating them like valued customers. Recruitment processes are managed by unimaginative recruiters for whom the word "business" holds no special meaning.

First of all, **it is no understatement to define the role of the corporate recruiter as the Chief Talent Prevention Officer.** Unfortunately, many job seekers are led to believe that recruiters and recruitment processes are for their benefit. Too often, job seekers fail to define what "recruitment" is – and more importantly, what it is not. According to businessdictionary.com, **recruitment is** *"the process of identifying and hiring the best-qualified candidate (from within or outside of an organization) for a job vacancy, in a most timely and cost-effective manner."* Based on this definition, the recruitment process is not about finding jobs for applicants, but about finding the "best qualified candidates" for jobs. Job seekers would do well to understand that each organization has its own definition for what constitutes the "best-qualified candidate". Now, let's talk about what **"recruitment" is not.** Recruitment is not a hard science. Nor is it a liberal art. To my knowledge, there is no Newton's Law of Recruitment. There is no formula that exists for plugging in the characteristics of a potential employee, and predicting his work success with 100% accuracy. Universities don't offer Bachelors or Master's degrees in Recruitment. Therefore, I'm confident you won't meet anyone who tells you that he has just completed his Doctoral degree in Corporate Recruitment.

You don't need a professional license to be a recruiter. In reality, the recruiter can be anyone, and no one. What does all this mean? It means there is a lot of variance in recruitment practices from person to person, company to company, industry to industry, and country to country. Some people have extensive training and experience in recruitment, while others don't. Some people involved in the recruitment process have various university degrees and work experience, while others hold no degrees or special training at all. Some companies have dedicated recruiters and defined recruitment processes, while many others have no recruiters at all – not to mention processes! When you submit your résumé online to a job posting, or send an unsolicited résumé by email, there is no way for you to verify who is going to actually read it – if anyone! This is a major roadblock in your path to advancing in the recruitment process in order to speak with a Hiring Manager, or anyone who could actually see the benefits you would bring to a department or business unit.

"The 'talent connection' enables you to enter your information once and apply to many positions. You may keep your information and résumé up to date and when a recruiter reads your résumé, it will always use the current version. Creating a profile also allows us to find current and future jobs that may suit you." – Qualcomm

Corporate recruiters are not social workers charged with improving your quality of life and well-being. They are paid by the company to find the potential employees who will keep the business going. They get evaluated by how many jobs they fill with the best candidates – not by how many job applicants get placed. This is how the corporate recruitment game is played each and every day, and this is how talent is prevented from entering the doors of your target companies. Recruiters attempt to determine who the "best candidates" are through the use of artificial processes that are based on flawed designs and expectations. There is a serious problem when the selection of talent is more focused on form than function, but that is the reality of the corporate recruitment process. Recruiters are more concerned with controlling which applicants get selected and hired than with improving the function of the recruitment process for the average job seeker. The function of recruitment should be focused on creating processes for interested students and graduates to demonstrate how they can impact a company's business – not how they can apply for jobs online. Unfortunately, recruiters are more concerned with tweaking the existing form of their standard recruitment processes than on improving the outcomes of its intended function.

To understand the fundamental reasons for the lack of transparency in the corporate recruitment process, job seekers must first understand the fundamental problem: corporate recruiters. They are the invisible and faceless staff that companies inexplicably deploy to select and screen the lifeblood of the organization. Their identities are a mystery that you'll never solve unless you're (un)lucky enough to be contacted by one for an initial interview. Until that time, you'll have better luck spotting a magical unicorn, or the Loch Ness monster! Recruiters are not the Masters of the Universe they'd like to be recognized as, and most of them barely understand the businesses in which they work. There is no way the average corporate recruiter can discern a top job seeker from a bottom feeder without first having business experience in the department for which he is recruiting. Yet, again and again, you will be faced with the task of designing your résumés and other application materials with the express intent of passing the judgment of these inept recruiters. They are the Gatekeepers of Talent Acquisition and they happily peruse their turbo-charged applicant tracking systems each week to see who made it past their carefully-designed "talent" screens. This is more akin to Talent Prevention than Talent Acquisition, and the sooner you make the distinction, the better off you'll be in the game.

Another fundamental issue with the vast majority of corporate recruiters is that they are woefully incompetent to do the jobs they are paid to do. Of course, you can always have a bit of luck and come across the small minority of competent recruiters who actually work in the business departments for which they recruit (as well as having functional business experience in the functions for which they recruit) – but I wouldn't count on it. Most companies just don't seem to value the recruitment department enough to upgrade it with business-minded talent. Yet, these same companies obviously entrust these recruiters to select business-minded employees – go figure! There are two types of corporate recruiters you'll have the (dis)pleasure of speaking with if your online application is selected for an initial interview. The fundamental differences between the two will dictate what type of response you can expect from your application.

1. **The Incompetent.** Without question, the majority of corporate recruiters are incompetent, and shamefully, will be the ones who hold the most power over who gets selected during the recruitment process. They are the "pure breeds" of Human Resources (HR) spawn: meaning their education and experience are deeply rooted in HR-related functions. They have no clue on how to measure talent other than what their applicant tracking systems tell them are the highest-ranked résumés matching the corresponding job postings. They are unable to see beyond the words on a résumé or application. They are unable to make inferences on how particular job applicants could be of value to the company even if they don't fit specific job postings. In fact, they are unable to understand the concepts of basic business, and remain warmly snuggled in the confines of their HR office. They rarely see (if ever) the business managers whom they support, and have no understanding of how to conduct an in-depth job analysis that will be reflected in the jobs they post. Their focus is on screening you out versus filtering you in: they will focus on putting you under the spotlight to question why you applied and what salary you expect. These recruiters are indeed a sore on the "corporate body" that is simply festering at your expense. It is not their job to try to find a job for you – no matter how talented you are. **Their only concern is to find the applications that best match the job postings fed into their applicant tracking systems.** They are incapable of connecting the dots on their own and are loathe to collaborate with business-minded Hiring Managers. If you've invested hours in constructing your résumé and cover letter, don't expect any return on that investment if you are being sourced by one of these recruiters.

2. **The Competent.** Somewhere hidden within the walls of major corporations are a few, intelligent, business-minded professionals who are employed as the corporate recruiters you can only dream about having as the owners of the Talent Acquisition Process. They are not spawns of HR, and usually move into corporate recruiting from other functional areas of

the business of which they have an in-depth understanding. These professionals are concerned with getting the right person into the organization that will impact identified business metrics. **They have the ability to see through smoke-screen résumés and look for the tiny nuggets of information about job seekers that an applicant tracking system can't decipher.** Their business instinct enables them to easily discern who are the best application writers and interviewers, versus who are the most competent applicants and resource people. These recruiters have intimate relationships with the business units they serve, and sit in the same weekly meetings as the rest of the Hiring Manager's team – their clients and stakeholders. Their functional business knowledge makes them a valued asset and a trusted source capable of deciphering the type of competencies needed to satisfy the needs of their clients. These recruiters understand both the short-term and long-term needs of the organization, and will screen your application materials with that in mind. Even if your profile isn't the best fit for the jobs to which you applied, these recruiters are smart enough to determine if you have valuable skills that could be beneficial to solving other business challenges (present and future). In short, competent recruiters don't try to fit job seekers to the job posting: they try to fit them to the organization. If you have taken the time to define your value as a resource person, and communicate it effectively, then keep your fingers crossed and pray that these recruiters contact you.

Chapter 4
Hiring Managers: The Ugly, The Bad, And The Good

"What are the steps in the hiring process? If we determine you meet the qualifications of a current opening, a member of our Human Resources team will contact you to schedule a time to discuss your background, experience, interest and the current opening. If it seems that the position may be a good fit for you, we'll schedule you for interviews with other individuals related to this position." – Target

The above quote is a clear and present reminder of who controls the hiring process – and it's not the Hiring Managers! The Hiring Managers decide who gets hired, but they don't manage (or control) the process that ferries the best job applicants (or application writers) to their office. As a job seeker, you can only hope and pray that you get past the corporate recruiters – and on to the Hiring Managers. If you could speak directly to your potential boss (the Hiring Manager), would you still want to interview with a recruiter? That is the question you have to ask yourself before starting the job search odyssey. The two main actors in the formal recruitment process are the corporate recruiters and the Hiring Managers. Understanding how each of them performs, and what they prioritize, is key to understanding why the rules of the corporate recruitment game are designed for the masses to fail – and fail miserably! Hiring Managers are not only responsible for hiring: they are actual Business Managers who have business goals and objectives for the departments they oversee. Don't think of them as corporate managers who are sitting around in top hats with rubber stamps just mindlessly deciding who gets extended an employment offer and who doesn't.

The term, "Hiring Manager", is just the moniker to use for the person who has the ultimate decision-making authority over who gets hired. However, you will rarely be given any clues to who this person is at your target employers when you get drawn into the formal recruitment process. It is not surprising that many job seekers are clueless about the construct of the recruitment game. You've been led to believe that corporate recruitment is an egalitarian process created for your benefit. Wrong! The process is designed to shield Hiring Managers – the ones who actually run the business – from being overwhelmed with the planning and administration involved with sourcing and recruiting their own talent. This construct curbs the power of the Hiring Managers, and relegates them to playing a minor role in hiring people for their own departments. By fault or design, this practice has become ingrained in the corporate recruitment process by the Human Resources department since they took over the responsibilities for guarding the gates of employment. To that end, HR is able to control the recruitment process by being the tail that wags the dog. **The entire recruitment process is designed to control which job applicants will be presented to the Hiring Managers.**

"Applications for all positions across Europe are handled by our recruitment team in Berlin, however your interview day is always held at the BASF site you have applied to. If you have any questions, the recruitment team will be happy to help at any time." – BASF

Let's be clear on one thing: Hiring Managers are not anti-talent people! In most cases your problem will not be with the Hiring Managers: it will be with the corporate recruiters who have assumed the duties of the Hiring Manager. In theory (only in theory!), removing the Talent Selection Process from the auspices of the Hiring Managers (business managers) might be plausible if a company believed that talent selection was not essential to running its business. However, the talent selection process is every bit as important as any other business process: it's the right employees who decide the success or failure of a company. It is rare to find companies smart enough to embed corporate recruiters within the business units they serve, as well as obliging that they have functional and industrial experience for the types of jobs they source. Somewhere along the talent selection continuum, a bean counter perhaps thought it better to centralize corporate recruiting, and move recruiters as far as possible from the business units for which they were hired to add value. That aberration became the norm across the majority of major corporations, and now it is a systemic problem that HR departments are all too happy to keep in place. Lost in all of this madness is the original client: the Hiring Manager. Remember, they are the business people – not the recruitment policy wonks.

Fortunately, Hiring Managers are not tied to the same rules as recruiters when it comes to sourcing and selecting talent. In fact, most (if not all) Hiring Managers detest HR types as much as job seekers do. Unfortunately, they too are held hostage by the HR department's stifling talent selection policies and practices, and will usually just go along with business as usual in order to keep the peace. Most Hiring Managers have one objective, and one objective only: hire competent people. Most recruiters have the singular objective of selecting the applications that best match the job postings. Nevertheless, it will be a mistake to believe that all Hiring Managers are business-minded individuals who are capable of sourcing and selecting their own talent. In some cases, Hiring Managers can be worse than the corporate recruiters who serve them! **There are Hiring Managers who are incapable of understanding their own business needs, and therefore are incapable of understanding how you could be of value to them.** You will be tasked with trying to discern the ugly, the bad, and the good Hiring Managers involved in the corporate recruitment process.

1. **The Butts In The Seat Hiring Manager.** These individuals are more concerned with quantity than quality and usually relinquish control of the entire recruitment process to HR. They are clueless about what their talent needs are, and even more clueless about the businesses they run. As their name suggests, their only concern is getting a body – anybody – to do a job. If you have the (mis)fortune to speak with them during the recruitment process, don't expect to receive any in-depth, meaningful questions about your fit for the job. As long as you can breathe and walk upright, you'll more than likely get a job offer: although the job you get won't be anything to write home about. These are the worst Hiring Managers of all, and probably cost their companies more money than they're

worth. **Instead of "doing business" that creates value, they "play business" that destroys value.** They view all job applicants the same regardless of talent level, and will not try to align your ksa's with the jobs you can do best. As such, you'll probably wish you were talking to an incompetent recruiter rather than these "firefighting" managers. Their lack of business acumen and lack of recruitment discipline will only serve to screw you even more than the entire recruitment process itself!

2. **The Tale Wags The Dog Hiring Manager.** These individuals let HR dictate their talent needs at the expense of selecting the right applicants. Even though they know it's wrong, they either feel powerless to stand up and do anything about it, or satisfied to let someone else handle their dirty work. **They will leave their fates in the hands of HR's due process and only interview the stiffs sent by recruiters.** These managers are lazy and hands-off in the sense that they'd rather another department be responsible for the sourcing of their job vacancies. They are usually happy to let HR shoulder that burden while they sit back and cherry pick the applicants screened by recruiters. Even if they meet a job seeker with a high-potential background outside of the formal recruitment process, they'd simply redirect that person to the appropriate recruiter for screening and processing. How dumb is that? These managers are little more than surrogate recruiters, and it will be hard to differentiate the two. They'll ask the same dumb questions as incompetent recruiters and you'll feel like you're in part one of the recruitment process all over again. These Hiring Managers rarely formulate their own unique questions outside of what HR instructs them to ask. For them, the recruitment process is just a "meet and greet" affair since they have relinquished their real power to HR lackeys.

3. **The Business-To-Business Hiring Manager.** These individuals don't trust HR and prefer to find their own talented employees. You won't be asked dumb questions by these managers so you'd better be ready for a real interview –

or business discussion. These managers do not use recruiters in any way to source, screen, or select the employees for their departments. Instead, they only use recruiters to finalize the details of the hiring paperwork. If you are lucky enough to be contacted directly by these Hiring Managers, it means you won't have to deal with the cheese-grater screens that incompetent recruiters would make you go through. It means that you can truly concentrate on discussing (and demonstrating) why you should be extended an employment offer. **These managers are mainly concerned about your ability to make the company money and save the company money.** Therefore, don't expect any standard interview questions to get thrown your way. They prize creativity and ingenuity, and will look for those traits in everything you do. Time is money to these managers so playing "musical chairs" is a waste of their time. They will judge you on your business acumen, proposed solutions, and likeability. These managers will extend you an employment offer if, and only if, you are able to demonstrate your competence.

Chapter 5
Online Application Versus Private Investigation

"We conduct a Criminal Background Check, Education Verification and Drug Screen. Some positions also require a motor vehicle check. All portions of the check must be completed before you can begin employment." – American Express

Global corporations behave in strange ways: much like secret societies that only want to accept members of a certain pedigree. These members-only clubs go to great lengths to ensure the purity of their bloodlines by not accepting the wrong member. In this respect, corporations resemble monarchies desiring to groom possible successors to the throne (or to important leadership positions throughout the kingdom). To be selected as a job candidate means that you will have to exhibit certain characteristics through the information you disclose on the online application. Recruiters will inspect your personal, professional, and academic lineage for any vestiges of corporate royalty. The name of the game is to find the potential crown-princes hidden among the masses of applicants; however, they are still looking for officers and gentlemen to take care of the daily administrative tasks. This is the key role played by the online application in the corporate recruitment game: the information you are requested to submit is essential to a recruiter's ability to screen your profile for any hints of nobility – or serfdom. If your application is flagged for additional follow up, then you can expect that recruiters will begin a private investigation on the details you submitted at some point during the recruitment process: only you won't know exactly what that investigation entails.

Job seekers rarely have a clear definition of the component parts of the corporate recruitment game as it pertains to how the information submitted online is used in the recruitment process. It is indeed a very opaque process that lacks the transparency of an open system, even though we are living in an era of increased calls for openness and transparency in government, academia, and corporations. When you begin an online job application the game instantly switches to a mode of converting you into measurable bits of data. This is done by intelligent software that analyzes the details of the information you submit (including the results of pre and post-application tests). You are obliged to certify that the information you submit is truthful, otherwise you can be excluded from further consideration. However, don't expect for companies to return the favor by providing you with detailed truthful information regarding their job postings and workplace environment. Completing an online application is designed to be a one-way evaluation where the recruiters only look to receive your information – not give you theirs. The fact that global corporations have been able to successfully continue this practice is a testament to the power of their employer branding campaigns. Why else would highly-competent job seekers continue to participate in a one-side-tells-all application process?

For many reasons, not least of which is public scrutiny, companies are not forthcoming with specific employment details that should be made available to job seekers before and after the application submission. The decision to apply online should not be taken lightly given the time investment and adverse risks to your career should you make a bad employment decision that could have been avoided. It is indeed ironic that companies themselves do all they can to avoid making a bad hiring decision by basically stripping away all your rights to privacy in order to access your prior and current employment records. But what recourse do you have to get access to the transparent details of a company's employer value proposition? None! Your best defense in this situation is to have a clear understanding of why companies want your information and how it will be used throughout the recruitment process. Once you submit your application, that information can and will be used against you throughout the recruitment process. Recruiters will have unfettered access to check your credentials using non-transparent methods: some will push the ethical boundaries with your former employers and references by asking off-the-record questions (even if their own companies have policies in place that prohibit such practices). There will be no official transcripts of the conversations and no way for you to verify what will be said – or not said.

"If you are selected for the position, your employment will be contingent upon submission to and successful completion of a post-offer/pre-placement drug and alcohol screening as well as pre-placement verification of the information and qualifications provided during the selection process." – BP

Many online applications purposely confine the information you submit into standardized templates to make it easier for recruiters to compare and contrast you against other applicants. Instead of requesting that you submit information that supports your case to be considered a job candidate, recruiters are more concerned with collecting superficial data that have nothing to do with your ability to add value to their companies. In some cases, they will even request your social security number! What possible reason could any recruiter have for wanting the most personal identification number there is from a job seeker who has not even been selected for further consideration? If it is just for the purpose of assigning a unique identifier to a submitted job application, then there are plenty of other numbers that can be used – not to mention random numbers that can be generated by the applicant tracking system. Nowadays, companies have gone a step further by obliging you to electronically sign a "data request" waiver before you are even allowed to begin a job application – an unscrupulous practice! Why should you be expected to be so careless with your personal information when you have no clue if you will even be selected for an interview or extended an employment offer? Companies do not need all of your personal details before deciding whether or not they want to give you an initial interview; however, they will attempt to convince you otherwise by not offering any alternatives to their application requirements.

Given the frequent security breaches compromising the personal accounts of customers/clients stored in corporate databases (i.e. Citibank, Sony, etc.), you should think twice before divulging any applicant information you would not want made public – especially if the information is irrelevant to your ability to do the job. Most recruiters will never tell you when (or if) they will conduct a background check on your submitted application. Therefore, all your personal details could just be sitting in some database whose level of security is not made known to you. Besides that, you are not given the option to delete your own application from the company's database if you are not selected for an interview. Job seekers are at the mercy of a company's policy on background checks as well as its information security policies on submitted applications. At the very least, recruiters should tell you their policies and practices on conducting background checks. Some say that they only conduct post-employment offer checks; however, they don't specify exactly what that means. Others say they will conduct pre-placement verification checks; however, they provide very little information as to what that includes. This lack of transparency shields recruiters from public scrutiny, and allows them to conduct clandestine background checks at your expense.

Why should job seekers be obliged to submit salary details, social security numbers, and contact information for ex-bosses on the job application? Furthermore, why should they have to take psychometric tests – and sometimes authorize credit report checks – as part of the application? It's all part of the process that allows recruiters to screen and select job applicants against non-transparent criteria. The online application is essential to the functioning of the corporate recruitment game. It is the only mechanism that allows recruiters to digitize your entire personal and professional profile without ever having to speak to you. It is the means by which the corporation can establish baselines for the selection of the next crop of corporate employees. There is absolutely no advantage gained by you when you submit an online application because you will never be given an official document showing how that information was used. Ask any competent Hiring Manager what are the key characteristics they look for in employees and they will list only a small percentage of the information collected by recruiters from the online application. In reality, the only information that recruiters and Hiring

Managers need during the pre-employment offer stage is proof that you meet the basic requirements of the job posting. Nevertheless, you'll need to understand how the applicant information you submit is used against you.

1. **Signed Release Statement For Prior Employers.** Many companies will request that you sign away your rights that prohibit prior employers from divulging certain information about you. Unfortunately, you are not privy to exactly what information they will seek from those employers. Companies can request your performance ratings, salary history, supervisor's opinions, and other details depending on your prior employers' information release policy. What does all this mean? Any details that recruiters receive about you won't be shared with you. Since you won't know exactly what information the recruiter will request, or what will be said about your past performance and character, your advancement in the recruitment process can either proceed or be derailed. There is no law that obliges companies to share with you the details of the information given to them by your prior employers. Therefore, it's in your best interest to contact your prior employers to learn their information release policies.

2. **Salary History, Current Salary, Expected Salary.** A lot of companies ask you to provide your salary details during the application process. Some have been known to even ask for prior (or current) pay stubs in addition to the prior year's tax returns. If you get selected for a telephone-screening interview, you will most certainly be asked about your salary details. It's ironic that these companies almost never provide you with the salary details for their jobs, yet they obsess about having yours. What does all this mean? If you are transparent with your salary details, then you leave yourself vulnerable to a recruiter's (and Hiring Manager's) biases and interpretation of whether your salary is outside their unstated range. You can be excluded from the process if your current salary (and expected salary) is perceived to be too high – or too low.

Worse than that, you can be pegged to a salary far below the value you'd bring to the company.

3. **Recruitment and Selection Tests.** More and more companies are relying on the so-called "objective" data from various psychometric tests they require you to take during the completion of the online application or afterwards if you make it past the initial screening interviews. What does all this mean? Recruiters will determine your *knowledge, skills, and abilities* based on your test scores for the particular test they use: the results of which may never be made known to you. Regardless of your experience and prior accomplishments, companies will use their test scores as the overriding validation of your talents. Depending on how you do on the test, this can work for you or work against you. But who wants their job candidacy to be decided by a standardized test that can't possibly simulate how you would actually perform on the job?

4. **Consumer Credit Checks.** It's all about quantifiable numbers and your credit score communicates something about you (perceived or real) that recruiters and Hiring Managers can use to make a decision about you. The only problem is that you won't always be given an opportunity to explain any adverse detail on your report that might affect their decision to hire you or advance you in the recruitment process. What does all this mean? If you have a high credit score and little to no debt, then you'll be okay. But in the case where you have a high debt load, recruiters can make inferences about your character and personal finances. This also might not bode well for you during a salary negotiation since they'll know your financial obligations and needs. If you'll be in a job dealing with money, then they might be inclined to think that you'd be prone to theft or unethical behavior. It seems that major corporations have become the moral authorities on consumer debt. This is ironic given the fact that most companies are heavily indebted, and prone to engage in far more questionable financial practices than the average job

candidate: do Enron, Parmalat, Lehman Brothers, and MF Global ring any bells?

Do you think that you'll find the equivalent treasure trove of background information on a company's EVP? The only information you will be relegated to validating is the general information you find on a company's career site and employer review sites. Will recruiters give you the contact information for high-ranking former employees or recently terminated employees with whom you wish to speak? Will they tell you the salary ranges for the job postings to which you apply? Will they tell you the psychometric profiles of your potential co-workers? Don't hold your breath! Job seekers wanting mutual disclosure of key employment details are relegated to limited information that is almost never certified by the company or any third party agency. You'll need to thoroughly evaluate what an employer has disclosed in the public domain: their career website, job postings, annual reports, and sustainability reports at a minimum. Since companies don't take any oaths or sign any statements attesting to the truthfulness of their career-related information, you'll have to decipher their coded data based on your own reasoning and analysis. You really have no way to effectively decipher and interpret the code since it will vary from company to company. And worst of all, most of the employment information made public will contain a dearth of objective data!

It is easy for well-intentioned job seekers to misjudge their target employers and blindly apply online in hopes of landing their dream job. This is the construct of the corporate recruitment game: it draws you in under false pretenses, and then asks you to read the fine print. Any questions you might have about the recruitment process or the company's EVP will have to be put on hold. When you are reviewing job postings of interest and have questions about the requirements, who can you contact? Recruiters don't list any contact information for you. If you have questions about information on the company's career website, who can you contact? It's safe to say the webmaster probably isn't the right person. It's highly unlikely you'll be given the contact information for an actual recruiter or person with knowledge of the company's employment practices, policies, and programs. And even in the cases where you have the pleasure to speak directly to recruiters, how likely is it that they will be able to provide you with the details you want? It's not as if you'll be working for them if you get hired, and it's unlikely they will add to their already burgeoning workloads just to chase down information for your pleasure.

"Before you apply, be sure to research the industry and our firm. There's a wealth of information on this site and in the financial press. Then carefully and candidly consider your personal career goals and see if they match what J.P. Morgan has to offer." – J.P. Morgan

While the company is able to obtain the exact information it wants from you during the recruitment process, you'll have to settle for the poor man's version of the equivalent information you find on the company's website (and other public domains). **Companies expect you to believe the employment information they furnish, yet they clearly don't believe the information you furnish without verifying it through their pre-employment checks.** Companies only provide the information they are prepared to discuss with you. This significantly reduces the probability that you will find any red flags listed on their websites that would affect their employer reputation. Thus, you'll have to ask yourself whether everything that companies present to you is over-exaggerated at best, or over-simplified at worst. All of the words, pictures, videos, and podcasts about the "shiny, happy people" on a company's career site are no different than an advertisement commercial for a McDonald's hamburger: it always looks better than what you actually purchase. Employer branding hocus pocus is an ever-present force in the corporate recruitment game. You just have to know what it looks like, where is resides, and who it benefits the most – the corporate recruiter.

Chapter 6
Game Play: Cheat Codes, Hints, And Tips

"It's not wise to violate rules until you know how to observe them." – T. S. Eliot

The corporate recruitment game is like EA Sports: *"If it's in the game, it's in the game"*. But since job seekers are not privy to the game handbook, they are obliged to follow whatever instructions are laid out by recruiters. You will be played before you even start playing. Each move you make in the recruitment process has already been checkmated. They had you at hello, and will be more than happy to tell you good-bye if your job application is less than ideal. You started losing as soon as you started playing. There are major crossroads in the recruitment process that will serve to weaken your position if you advance. Though they may seem innocuous on the surface, their potency cannot be understated. In the recruitment game, nothing is as it seems, and every action you take has a hidden consequence. Throughout various stages of the formal recruitment process you'll be asked to answer key questions and to submit key information that is supposedly required for you to be considered a viable candidate. However, how you handle those stages will determine more than you realize about the outcome of your job search campaign.

It's easy to think that information you submit during the recruitment process can only bolster your candidacy to be selected and hired. While this may be true for some of the information, it is certainly not the case for all of it. The power in the recruitment game is tilted towards whoever has access to the most transparent information. **As soon as you apply online, you cede power to the recruiters because there won't be a mutual transfer of equivalent information.** It's like playing a game of poker where the recruiters keep their cards hidden, but they will know which cards you hold. If you reveal information during the game that does not aid your chances of winning, you'll effectively lose – even if you are extended an employment offer. You'll have to identify which information is absolutely necessary to evaluating your job candidacy, and which can be detrimental. In poker, every player has a *"tell"* that signals when he is bluffing. Job seekers who recognize the recruiters' tells will be able to call their bluff and win the hand.

"Each player must accept the cards life deals him or her: but once they are in hand, he or she alone must decide how to play the cards in order to win the game." – Voltaire

During the recruitment process, these tells take on many forms and job seekers have to recognize them in order to survive each stage and make it to the Big Boss at the end – the Hiring Manager. For each piece of information you are asked to submit, you need to use a cost-benefits analysis to determine: 1) is the information critical to supporting your job candidacy; 2) will failure to provide the information end your job candidacy; and 3) will submitting the information weaken your job candidacy. There are many indicators throughout the recruitment process that provide hints and warnings of the recruiter's attempt to trap you into a no-win situation. Below are examples of the major tells imbedded within the recruitment process, and how each one can negatively affect your employment candidacy.

1. **The Salary Discussion.** *"Please tell me your salary history?"* If a company does not ask you to state your salary details as part of the online application, then they will most certainly ask during the initial screening interview. No good can come from answering this question prematurely and it will completely ruin your negotiating position should you be extended an employment offer later. What does your salary history have to do with whether or not you are the right person for the job? Absolutely nothing! Companies engage in deceitful practice when they are not transparent with the salary ranges for their job postings. *"What are your salary expectations?"* This question obliges you to pick the right number to stay in the game, but if you pick the wrong number, you will be either low-balled or eliminated. The companies asking these questions are more focused on employee costs than employee value. Your fate

will be decided before you can even demonstrate your value-add to the company. Call their bluff! Do not answer any salary-related questions until you have more details about the job or are extended an employment offer.

2. **The Request For References And Ex-Bosses.** Why do companies request your references, and even try to dictate which ones you provide on the online application? You will never know the content of the conversation they have with these references. So how does that benefit you? You cannot assume that your references and ex-bosses will be able to provide the proper context for anything they say that might be viewed negatively. What may seem like a harmless statement from their standpoint could be detrimental to your job prospects. What if your last boss was not involved much in your daily work? What if you did not have a good relationship with him? Don't put yourself in a position where your job candidacy is decided based on someone else's subjective statements. There is no impartial judge who will instruct the recruiters to disregard any controversial or inadmissible statements. Call their bluff! The only time you should give any reference information is after you have been extended an employment offer. And even then, you need to clarify what questions the company will be asking so that you can provide them with your selected references – not theirs.

3. **The Company Loyalty Assessment.** *How long would you stay with our company?* Recruiters and Hiring Managers ask this question as if they are handing out lifelong employment contracts. They know the realities of the job market and how their companies are terminating masses of employees even as they bring new ones on board: so who are they trying to deceive? If you say that you want to stay with the company for the rest of your career, then you will be perceived as naïve and not prepared for the realities of the global market. If you say that you would like to commit as long as there is mutual growth and interest, then you will be categorized as a job hopper or non-committal. The loyalty assessment is just a

cover for the fact that companies want to be in control of when you are hired and fired. Recruiters will not tell you about their company's record on terminating employees, cutting salaries and benefits, and closing departments. Call their bluff! It would behoove you to know more about their loyalty towards employees rather than telling them how loyal you will be as an employee. Find out the details of their voluntary and involuntary turnover. The companies most concerned about how long you will stay are usually the ones who treat their employees the worst.

If job seekers knew the unwritten rules of the corporate recruitment game, then the majority probably would not even apply online. Recruiters rely on your ignorance to continue luring you into their preferred process for assessing your job candidacy. The more applications they have in their databases, the less work they have to do to sort talent when they need it – albeit not when you need a job. If you decipher the code used by the recruiters, you'll be able to discern when it is best to apply, and when it's best to walk away. Learn the language of recruiters and you'll make smarter choices. It is just as important to interpret what is said versus what is not said during the life-cycle of the recruitment process. Recruiter speak has double meanings and will negatively affect your success should you decide to apply online. However, in order to decipher the code you will first need to know where it is hidden.

1. **The Job Posting.** How is it that a company is able to specify the years of experience required to do a job? Furthermore, since when did job performance correlate to an arbitrary number of work years? That is just an example of the code you will find embedded within most job postings. A healthy dose of critical thinking skills are required to decipher the nonsensical text and corporate jargon you will find. Take time to analyze what the company is really communicating about the job and about its employer value proposition. Pay special attention to the terms used to describe the required experience, education, competence, and attitude. If any of

them seem incongruent, it's probably best that you don't apply. Some postings list statements such as, *"only local candidates will be considered"* or *"only candidates living within a 50 mile radius will be considered"*. I guess these recruiters have confined their talent pool to a restricted area, or they are too incompetent to just state, *"No relocation assistance"*.

2. **The Email Rejection Letter.** No one likes rejection, but a little common courtesy would at least ease the disappointment. Some letters will state, *"We have selected another candidate whose credentials are better suited to this position."* So does that mean your credentials hold no value for any other jobs in the company? Regardless of where in the process you get rejected, the code words used by the recruiter are very important. Some rejection letters have the audacity to tell you to continue searching for jobs on the company's site. Yeah right, as if that worked out so well the first time. If a recruiter is not smart enough to recognize your talent from the first application, I highly doubt it is worth your time to send successive applications. If the recruiter values your profile, then the smart thing for him to do would be to find a place for you within the company – even if it was not for the job posting to which you applied. When a recruitment process fails to recognize your value, but requests that you keep applying, then the game is over.

3. **The Interview.** During interviews, recruiters and Hiring Managers might ask you questions that focus heavily on your past accomplishments. But isn't the objective of an interview to find out if you can do the job for which you applied? If you find that you're being asked too many standard cookie-cutter questions about your past experience, then the recruiter might have already decided your fate. If interviewers are hesitant to give you any immediate feedback regarding your prospects to advance in the recruitment process, then that is not a good sign. Think about it, if you find a one-of-a-kind item on eBay that you really want, will you hesitate to buy it outright – or at least bid on it? That same logic holds true during interviews. If

a recruiter (or Hiring Manager) has no sense of urgency regarding your candidacy, then it means that they are just not that into you. It doesn't mean that you are not still a viable candidate; however, it does mean that you are not the ONE.

4. **The Career FAQ's.** A treasure trove of recruiter code can be found in the frequently asked questions (FAQ) section of the career site. Many FAQ's will state, *"due to the high volume of applications received we are unable to respond to each applicant"*. That can be translated to mean that the company does not place any importance on providing feedback to unwanted job applicants. You will be lucky if you even receive a rejection email! What incentive do you have to apply unless you are reasonably assured that you will get a favorable reply? It's not as if you're just applying to jobs out of boredom. You will also find statements such as *"only applicants fitting the desired profile will be contacted"*, and *"we aim to get back to candidates within two weeks of an interview"*. That does not sound too inviting to job seekers who really want a job. Take time to review the FAQ's to assess the company's transparency regarding the details of their recruitment process.

Companies do not pull punches in the corporate recruitment game and will play as dirty as a fighter in a no-holds barred cage match. They will influence you through psychological warfare by using tactics that would put Maslow's "hierarchy of needs" to shame. Employer branding hocus pocus (EBHP) is used to appeal to your emotions and the things you value. Savvy advertisers know that the best way to sell a product is to appeal to consumers' basic needs of safety, security, and status. Employer branding campaigns replicate these tactics and keep you marching in unison with the rest of the job seekers clamoring for a spot in the online application line: all with hopes of becoming the next corporate employee bestowed with the safety, security, and status they have been led to believe it entails. EBHP is oftentimes subtle and borders on the subliminal: you won't always see billboard advertisements extolling the virtues of working for company X.

Nonetheless, it is an ever-present force in the game and reaches you even when you are not actively playing.

"If candidates are interested in your organization, you may want to convert them into believing you are a desirable employer – a company profile or inside story in a student career magazine, or one-on-one meetings to interact with potential candidates, for example, will certainly be effective." – www.employerbrandingtoday.com

"Recruitment marketing refers to the process of attracting candidates to employers through the process of posting jobs and employment branding initiatives. The marketing aspect comes into play with recruiting when a recruiter is asked to "sell" both the company and job order through the web copy of the job order and any and all information about the company and the employment experience." – www.recruiter.com

Without EBHP, the entire corporate recruitment game would come to a screeching halt: leaving only the undesirable job seekers with incentive to apply. The game is all about global companies' obsession to attract the best and the brightest in order to accomplish three goals: 1) further the companies' business plans; 2) hoard them from the competition; and 3) keep them from starting competing firms. Job seekers will need to discern when they are being a pawn in some company's game by carefully judging its employer value proposition (EVP) against objective criteria. In Part Four of this book, I give details on how to judge the EVP of your target companies so that you don't fall prey to their unrelenting shenanigans. Companies that have popular product brands get the added bonus of using them as surrogate employer brands. Many job seekers find themselves so enamored with the company's products that they will just readily accept the shallow information the company states about its EVP…and readily enter a formal recruitment process designed to prune the masses.

Chapter 7
Confessions Of A Corporate Recruiter

"Writing is the only trade I know of in which sniveling confessions of extreme incompetence are taken as credentials probative of powers to astound the multitude." – George V. Higgins

It is not often that job seekers get proof of the corporate recruitment game's existence. The game itself has almost become an urban legend thanks to the massive use of EBHP to obscure its existence. Nonetheless, the game is indeed alive and well, and thriving under covert operations. When you do advance in the recruitment process, but get rejected at a later stage, you're usually left clueless as to why. Of course, most corporate recruiters will never give you any feedback as to why they rejected you, other than to tell you the standard company line: *"We found a candidate that better matched the requirements of the job."* I was able to find candid feedback from a corporate recruiter who stepped out of the shadows to give a personal testimony. Although the majority of corporate recruiters will never admit to it, her words ring true for how they behave in thought, word, and deed. Pay special attention to the jargon used by this recruiter so that you can recognize it during your own job search campaign.

"Forgive me, job search candidates, for I have sinned. It's been 20+ years since my last confession. I ran recruiting efforts for Fortune 500 firms that included Citigroup, Warner-Lambert, and most recently Merrill Lynch and during that time, I committed many sins. I seek atonement through this article.

<u>Sin #1</u>: *I made instant judgments about what types of candidates they would be in the first three seconds I met them. It's true, I sized them up. I'm guilty.*

I wanted to tell them that they should have tried that suit on two days before the event, so they could have gotten that stain off of their tie or jacket. I wanted to tell them to look me in the eye versus over my left shoulder. I wanted to tell them to use breath mints, because they were leaving dead bodies in their wake.

But alas, I sinned and said nothing. I just selected the candidates that had polish, that prepared, that took care in their appearance from their hair to their nails to their shoes.

<u>Sin #2</u>: *When candidates asked why they didn't make the cut, I never truly answered them. Instead, I avoided any potential litigation and simply said "It was a competitive process."*

I lied. I didn't tell them they didn't answer my questions directly, or completely, or enthusiastically, or in a "results oriented" way. I didn't tell them that they should have clearly identified how they solved problems for their past employers – how they eased their pain! I didn't tell them that I heard negative comments in their responses to my questions because any mention of anything negative will immediately shift me to the next candidate. I didn't tell them it was because they were five minutes late to the interview and I feared they would be late to a client meeting as well.

Instead, I sinned and gave no feedback. It wasn't my job to give them feedback. It was my job to hire the best candidates who mastered the art of the interview and who answered my questions directly, effectively and in a results oriented manner. I hired the person who proved why they would be indispensable to my firm.

<u>Sin #3</u>: *When I asked the question, "tell me about your strengths", and "tell me about your weaknesses", if a candidate looked like they hadn't a clue, I would move on to the next person. If they aren't self-aware, they could never truly improve as an individual. And I didn't hire anyone who wasn't in a constant state of improvement.*

I sinned and said nothing. I didn't give feedback, because it wasn't my job to do so. It was my job to award the job to the person who did a self-assessment in a meaningful way. I hired the person who invested in being the best interview candidate possible.

Sin #4: If candidates didn't maintain good eye contact, I silently shouted "NEXT!" in my head. If they didn't look me in the eye when they shook my hand, they received a negative mark right off the bat!

I wanted to tell them how body language speaks so loudly that I can't hear what they are saying, and that the more you looked me in the eye, the more I trusted what you had to say.

But I sinned and said nothing. Instead, as they looked over my shoulder while talking to me, I turned to see if there was someone behind me. There never was.

Sin #5: If a candidate didn't ask good, thoughtful questions at the end of the interview, I went on to the next candidate. Not having insightful questions shows a lack of preparation and interest. It's a rookie mistake that I won't overlook.

I wanted them to know that a little research goes a long way. They could have walked into the interview with 5 – 7 questions written down on their portfolio pad, and they could have easily referenced those questions at the end of the interview.

But my sin was my silence. I just hired those candidates that were thoughtful and prepared, and that impressed me with their questions.

My atonement has been found in my past three years as a career coach. I tell the truth now: the good, the bad and the ugly, so candidates can improve, and so they can launch effective and successful job searches. My clients can now find the job of their dreams because I give them immediate tactical and strategic feedback from my 20+years of hiring thousands of individuals. I can rest easier now as my clients are landing the jobs they want. Amen." – Connie Thanasoulis

Part Two

Corporate Recruiters Do The Recruiting

Chapter 8
The Traditional Job Search

"A smart man makes a mistake, learns from it, and never makes that mistake again. But a wise man finds a smart man and learns from him how to avoid the mistake altogether." – Roy H. Williams

Even after reading the first few chapters of this book you will probably still feel the inevitable pull to waste the majority of your active job search applying to jobs online. **This is the traditional job search and it has been promoted as the *de facto* job search method for aspiring corporate employees.** What the sponsors of the traditional job search method don't tell you is that the corporate recruitment process is about employers' needs – not YOURS! It's not like companies want to speak with you first, learn all about your motivations, and then create a job just to suit your specific needs. You've been told throughout your academic and professional life to search for job postings – and what a frustrating search it can be during times of slow market growth. You have been told by companies to just go online and see what postings are there. You have been told by employers that they are not hiring. You have browsed job posting after job posting only to find a precious few for which you meet most of the requirements. You have even applied to jobs for which you were obviously under-qualified, and even overqualified; just hoping that someone, anyone, would have mercy upon your poor little résumé.

At this point, you have no shame – you just want a job! And any job will do. As you become more desperate, you lose all rationale and become a complete zombie who foolishly applies to job after job. Like an old failing company that refuses to change tactics, you search the Matrix of global job boards for the ONE. You know it is out there just waiting for you to stumble upon it like a pot of gold at the end of the rainbow. And so, on and on you go finding job posting after job posting: tirelessly sending your worn-out application to each one. If your résumé had feet, they would be gnarled and lumpy like the roots of an ancient sequoia tree! Trust me, by now the cyber world knows your name. You're the talk of the virtual town! Indeed, you've become quite popular. Only you don't get invited to the exclusive parties. No, your name is not (and will never be) on the guest list. In fact, if your résumé shows up at the virtual door unannounced, it will be summarily executed! All the cyber gates that say "help wanted" are programmed to say "no vacancies" when they see your résumé. The only people who do want you (and are desperately seeking you) are the cyber sanitation engineers because they want to delete you from the résumé database!

Mindlessly sending your résumé into cyberspace is like spamming! And pretty soon the constantly evolving online application system will either filter you into the spam folder, or store you in the holding bin of a company's applicant tracking system...sadly awaiting a death row march towards the electronic trash bin. For too long, job seekers have been jilted at the altar of the online application process: asked to commit to an in-depth application, but usually left with no affirmative reply. Companies will never tell you how many job seekers are rejected daily by the system; let alone how many submitted applications are never even seen by an actual person. From the moment you conduct your job search with the intent to apply online, consider yourself plugged into the corporate recruitment game. The only problem is that most job seekers are ill-equipped to play the game and end up in the scrap heap of discarded applications. Remember, the game is designed to give corporate recruiters and Hiring Managers the advantage – not you.

"Once you apply for a job, your qualifications and experience will be reviewed by one of our recruiters to determine if you are a fit. If you are a possible match for the position, a recruiter will contact you to learn more about your background and answer questions about our hiring process and what it's like to work at Google." – Google

Virtually every corporation follows the standard recruitment model that relies on attracting potential candidates to apply for jobs online, and then separating the wheat from the chaff. The question you have to ask yourself is: *Who does this process favor?* Many job seekers naively believe that the recruitment process is a job matching process. They believe that the sheer number of job postings translates to an increased probability of being contacted for an interview –and eventually extended an employment offer. This could not be further from the truth. The probability of being contacted is dependent upon a number of independent variables that are outside of your control. Furthermore, it is not even possible for you to assess your chances of being contacted given the opaqueness of the recruitment process. You will never know the number of qualified applicants applying for the same job. You will never know if there is already an identified internal candidate. You will never know if your application was thoroughly assessed by a competent person qualified to determine your value add.

Regardless of what I tell you about the corporate recruitment game, the lure of the online application is very seductive. Recruiters will always encourage you to search for job postings online. It's fast, it's easy, and it's the recruiter's law – at least, that's what they would like for you to believe. When you apply online, it allows recruiters to control and dictate every aspect of how you present yourself as a candidate of choice. There will be little room for you to differentiate yourself beyond the standard documents of the traditional résumé and cover letter. Job seekers are required to show obeisance to the application rules, and any act of disobedience will be met with a swift rejection from the recruitment process. Before you dutifully obey the letter of the recruiter's law, there are a few details you need to know about the principles of the lawmakers:

1. **Recruiters DO NOT Care About Your Job-Search Anxiety.** A harsh but true statement. But if you really think about it, why should they care? They don't even know you! It's like asking Johnny Depp to personally answer your fan mail. Sorry, it's not going to happen. You'll be lucky to receive a copy of an autographed photo if he has a good public relations office. And your average company definitely doesn't treat job applicants like movie star fans! Your average company does

not place any value on contacting every job seeker who applies to a job. They only place a value on contacting the ones they want to interview! Your job search is on your own timetable, not the company's. They didn't open a recruitment process just for you. And they most certainly won't rush to close the process because of you.

2. **Recruiters DO NOT Read Every Résumé You Submit.** But surely you already knew that, right? Surely you didn't think a recruiter's favorite hobby was to kick back in his favorite chair and read your résumé line by line like a best-selling novel. I know it's harsh, but believe me it is true. What recruiters like to do is "eyeball scan" résumés in as little time as possible to see if anything is worth following up on. Recruiters are in constant search for "The One" – the candidate whose résumé is the proverbial needle in a haystack. Many experienced recruiters take less than 20 seconds to review résumés. If you don't submit the "perfect" résumé, you might be better off if an inexperienced recruiter received it: assuming it even makes it past the résumé screening software.

3. **Recruiters' Lives DO NOT Revolve Around The Job Posting You Applied To.** No recruiter is spending his entire workday focused on the job posting that just happens to be the one to which you applied. Recruiters have multiple job postings to juggle, multiple job applicants to screen, and multiple interviews to conduct. Besides that, they also have to sit in meetings, go to lunch, take breaks, and complete a plethora of administrative duties related to recruitment activity. Oftentimes they are overworked, underpaid, and constantly behind on their schedules. It's not an envious lifestyle: it is one that is full of daily stress. So while you're sitting at home each day anxiously awaiting a response from the many jobs you've applied to online, the recruiter responsible for those jobs is unconcerned about your situation. Furthermore, he doesn't even have the time (or the inclination) to send you a standard rejection email.

Before you blindly follow the rules of the corporate recruitment process and make yourself cannon fodder for an unscrupulous game, you need to have a realistic overview of the process (chapters 9-15). Recruiters will not tell you the facts about what really goes on behind the scenes in the corporate recruitment game. Their mission in the game is clear: get you to apply online so that you can be dissected like a frog in an 8th grade biology class. And they will use every sleight of hand marketing tactic in the employer branding playbook to dupe you into believing that applying online is your best opportunity to be selected for an interview. Recruiters need only to guide your every step like a beacon from a lighthouse guiding a lost ship at night. You will only be allowed to see what recruiters want you to see, when they want you to see it. For a very small number of "special" job seekers, their quest to become a corporate employee will end in the land of milk and honey: indeed, they will be extended employment offers. For the rest, it will end in the land of salt and vinegar: indeed, they will be extended rejection letters (should the company be inclined to be so courteous). When using the traditional job search, each corporate career site you visit will further condition you to believe that somewhere over the rainbow awaits your dream job.

Chapter 9
Corporate Career Sites: Bait And Switch Advertising

"Explore the site and discover what we have to offer. By understanding how we work, you'll be better placed to decide if you want to apply. It will also help when you complete the application." – Unilever

The purpose of a corporate career site should be to engage and communicate with the job seekers who desire to evaluate a company's employment value proposition (EVP). After reviewing hundreds of career sites, it's clear that companies are behind the curve in utilizing them for a competitive advantage. Instead of providing the transparent details of their employer value proposition, most career sites just corral you towards their job search page. Thus, engagement with you is reduced to one-way communications with the companies shaping and coloring the lens through which they want you to view them. Very rarely will a career site offer the technology for a two-way conversation with someone knowledgeable of the company's EVP. Many career sites now make use of the major social media technologies, but only as a way for job seekers to connect with them – not the other way around. The majority of these efforts still focus mainly on pushing information out to job seekers *en masse* versus facilitating individual conversations. So while your goal is to evaluate a company's EVP before you apply, the company's goal is to get you to apply before you evaluate.

"There are a number of social media platforms/networks we will certainly leverage to market our employment brand. Through these channels we will build and engage talent communities and eventually stimulate direct applications." – www.hrmagazine.co.uk

The prevailing objective of most career site designs is to oblige interested job seekers to browse job postings on the job search page, apply online, and then speak to a recruiter later – provided they are not screened out by the applicant tracking system. Some career sites are little more than empty shells which take up space on a company's website. Others are so cluttered, or poorly-designed, that they are of little to no value. If the eyes are the window to the soul, then a corporate career site is the window to a company's workplace. It is often said that one should not judge a book by its cover, yet that is exactly what happens in practice when job seekers and corporate recruiters interact. Viewed another way, the career site of a company can be compared to the résumé of a job seeker. The former wants to entice you to complete an online application, the latter wants to entice recruiters to select you for an interview. Given the dearth of engaging career sites that provide useful information, it is not surprising why some savvy job seekers abandon the recruitment process altogether. Most companies use career sites to either over-sell their EVP or under-sell it: few, if any, get it just right. These companies create the most problems because they don't give you a realistic view of what to expect from their workplaces.

"To learn more about P&G, our people and our brands, check out our Website that gets right to the heart of the P&G career experience." – Procter & Gamble

"Welcome! This website will help you learn about General Mills, search and apply for available positions, and track the progress of your application. You'll find all sorts of helpful information here, from details about our culture to interview tips. We're excited to meet you!" – General Mills

The most technically advanced career sites attempt to compensate for their lack of transparent EVP data by providing you with addictive social media games or interactive virtual office tours. This will keep you distracted long enough to convince you that there is no need to investigate whether or not you should apply. Before long, you'll start searching for a job posting to take to the online checkout cart. A rational job seeker would not be in such a hurry to apply to a company whose EVP has not been thoroughly evaluated. You don't see companies hiring job seekers based on their résumés and applications alone, do you? Companies rely on your ignorance of the corporate recruitment game in order to keep you from asking the profound questions that any sensible job seeker would want to know before wasting their time. As an example, you only need to visit the "Investors" page found on a company's website to see how the career sites cheat you with their scarcity of certified, transparent data. Companies that hide more than they reveal regarding their EVP are the ones that need to bait you into applying online with embellished gibberish. Most companies only want to hoodwink you into believing that you have a fair chance to become an employee, when in reality, you don't.

Virtually all career sites display the same standard EVP information divided into four parts: 1) training; 2) benefits; 3) culture; and 4) career paths. The difference is only in how well they enshroud that information with deceptive marketing. On one end of the spectrum, you have companies that barely provide any details of their EVP –only stating that they have the basics. On the other end, you'll find companies that dress their career sites in Xbox-style graphics and social media-embedded games that could rival Farmville and Mafia Wars! But what you won't find is a simple, downloadable document that is the equivalent of the Annual Report that potential investors are privy to on the Investors page. This is why many companies invest heavily in employer branding so that you fall for the sleight of hand tricks that distract you from asking about the dearth of transparent EVP data on the career site. How many of the top job seekers would apply online if they could read a detailed EVP report on the career site? Judging the records of most global companies, it's fair to say that most of the high-potential job seekers would stay away altogether or demand higher compensation if extended an employment offer. It's far easier – and less costly – for companies to use fancy employer branding campaigns to attract top job seekers to apply than to invest in building a world-class EVP.

"You have unique experiences, skills and passions – and we believe you can bring them all to Microsoft for a rich, rewarding career and lifestyle that will surprise you with its breadth and potential. Just imagine the excitement and satisfaction of what you can do, where you can go, and the difference you can make with the resources of Microsoft behind you."
– Microsoft

Most career sites will attempt to sell you every possible aspect of the company's EVP whether it is true or not. It is all too easy to believe that what you see is what you get. But that can't be further from the truth. You are likely to find a full menu of every possible benefit the company deems worthy to answer the question: *Why should you work for us?* But don't let the presence of empty words and flash videos trick you into believing those benefits will be available to you. Career sites take their advertising cues from the rank and file retail stores that send you catalogs full of items: though the ones you want will always be out of stock. It is classic bait and switch, and it works almost every time because companies know that you have very few alternatives to learn about their EVP. Therefore, companies will use every side-street hustle to convince you that they are an employer of choice, and that their EVP is comparable to every other top company. That's hogwash! Even the companies with known reputations for being sweatshops have the audacity to state that they warmly embrace work-life balance.

If companies promote and sell aspects of their workplaces that they really do not value, then they are creating an expectations gap with you. The same is true when companies withhold workplace details that could aid your decision-making process. The more information you have at the initial point of engagement in the recruitment process, the better prepared you will be to ask the pertinent questions as to whether or not you wish to pursue the process. Information on a career site, like the information that job seekers put on their application and résumés, is expected to be truthful and transparent. When information on either of these representations of the company and the job seeker are found to be untrue, then both parties will suffer penalties. In your case, you can expect to be excluded from further consideration of employment. In the case of the company, it can expect that you will exclude it from further consideration. You won't find many career sites that have content worth judging: however, you will find a range of career sites that have focused more on their outward appearance versus their inner beauty. That being said, there are several categories of career sites that violate *"The Miss Universe Pageant's Protocol"* for career site design aesthetics.

1. **The Bells-And-Whistles Career Site.** If there was a prize awarded to the flashiest career sites in the world, these sites would win every year. They are replete with embedded videos of employee testimonies, virtual office tours, and online career finder assessments. Some have significantly reduced their written sales pitches while increasing the amount of information provided in interactive video formats. Others go a step further and engage you with online business games that allow you to learn the company's business through solving simulated challenges. While these career sites are highly engaging, creative, and interactive, they oftentimes fall short in providing any useful details on the company's EVP. These career sites are similar to the glitzy marketing campaigns that serve as cover for an inferior product. Despite all of these bells and whistles, you are still directed to complete an online application through the applicant tracking system just like any other drab career site. You will have to evaluate these companies by looking past the smoke and mirrors on their career sites to discover what EVP flaws they are covering.

2. **The Invisible Career Site.** Some companies go out of their way to hide their career sites. They hide the hyperlink in the smallest text possible in obscure locations on the company's home page. Sometimes the career site link can be found at the very bottom of the home page. Other times, it can be found under the "About Us" link (also written in the smallest possible text). This is especially true for companies that use their sites as e-commerce hubs (i.e., airlines and retail). For other companies that commit this error, it is probably an indication of the level of importance assigned to the talent acquisition process. When the career site is finally located, it is usually clear why it was hidden in the first place. It is oftentimes devoid of any useable content that would aid a job seeker's decision-making process. In the best case, these career

sites provide some basic workplace details. In the worst case, they link directly to the job search page. You will need to investigate the EVP of these companies through alternative channels in order to learn anything of value.

3. **The Ho-Hum Career Site.** Apparently, image isn't everything to these companies – at least not when it concerns job seekers. These career sites offer a stock photo here and there, but make no use of flash technologies or java script to create dynamic pages that engage you. They either offer pages of long, empty paragraphs; or pages of short, empty paragraphs. The career site menu usually consists of one link or several sub-links that provide only the most basic employment details. These sites do little to hold the attention of high-potential job seekers. The pages are not only dull in content, but also dull in presentation and appearance. They don't offer any compelling reason for you to stay on the site to investigate career opportunities. It's the equivalent of submitting a non-descript résumé that has no compelling headlines or information to capture the attention of the recruiter.

4. **The Hide-And-Seek Career Site.** Making important information difficult to find is probably not the best way for a company to develop rapport with job seekers. Yet, these career sites specialize in forcing you on an extended treasure hunt of the entire career site (and sometimes main company website) in order to locate pertinent information regarding the EVP. Instead of having client-focused menus and "related links" to relevant information, these sites just place career information haphazardly all over the website without any strategy or planning. These companies seem to give little thought to what you think about their employer brand. If you took this same approach and sent a résumé that buried key information all throughout the body of content, then the recruiter would quickly discard it. Why would a company be interested in speaking to job seekers who can't even write a client-focused – the recruiter and Hiring Manager being the clients – document? The same logic holds true for job seekers

researching corporate career sites. Why would high-potential job seekers be interested in applying to a company that cannot even produce a client-focused – you being the client – career site?

5. **The Lost-And-Found Career Site.** Navigating these career sites is like driving a car on a pitch-black road with no headlights. They do not provide any client-friendly options like a "drop-down menu", "pop-out menu", or "breadcrumbs" that allow you to easily see where you are on the website (and easily get back to the career site's main menu or some other section of the site). Each link either opens a new page with a different template or menu; or it opens into an entirely new site altogether. The worst offenders are the multinational companies that have multiple career sites: all with different career information and application methods. One wrong click and you can find yourself on an entirely different country's career site. The best you can do is to use your internet browser's back button or search for a career home page link. If you sent an online portfolio to a recruiter that provided no easy way for her to move from section to section without becoming lost, then she would probably not spend much time evaluating the content. I think it's safe to assume that you won't waste your precious time getting lost on a poorly-designed career site.

Career sites are one-way information highways that provide none of the information you expect to find to objectively evaluate an employer. They are no better than one-page fliers stuck on your windshield, stuffed into your mailbox, or handed out by sales agents. They are not designed for the purpose of facilitating personal interaction with anyone knowledgeable about the company's recruitment process and EVP. At most of the top ranked ideal employers, you will be hard-pressed to find an actual recruiter – let alone, a Hiring Manager – to engage with via the career site. Very few sites will provide you with any transparent information to aid you in properly evaluating their EVP. So how does the career site benefit you? Not much, really. Think of these career sites as the equivalents to advertisements for a retail store product: what is advertised versus what is sold won't be verified until you walk into the store. In the corporate world, it's highly unlikely that you'll be able to just enter the company of your choice and spend a day walking around the office to observe the workplace culture for yourself. Therefore, it is essential to understand that what you see on a career site is not always what you'll get in a work site.

Chapter 10
Job Postings: Confusion, Misdirection, And Disorder

"To apply for a job the first thing to do is choose a job posting that corresponds to you (in terms of your level of experience, the country in which you would like to work, the different families of jobs, etc.)" – Danone

When companies don't clearly state what they are looking for in a job posting, job seekers can't determine if the job corresponds to them or not. Companies demand coherent, focused, well-written résumés and cover letters from job seekers; but these same companies do not hold themselves accountable to those standards. Job postings are written with no concern about how their format and content reflect on the company. If the format and content of your résumé is viewed as a reflection of your communication skills, then the job posting also has to be viewed as a reflection of the company's communication skills. If a poorly written résumé was fortunate to make it past the applicant tracking system's screening tools, it would surely be rejected immediately by a recruiter without hesitation. Yet, day after day, recruiters advertise job postings that are filled with non-descript company jargon, demand a superhuman combination of skills and qualifications, or under-sell and understate the job's duties.

Companies have little incentive to invest in professionally-written job postings because the corporate recruitment game places the burden of professionally-written documents squarely on the job seeker. While it may be stressful for you to comb through Riddler-designed job postings, it's a joy for the recruiters who post them. Why? Because they know that only a small percentage of the job applicants will actually be converted into hires and the rest will be culled like flu-infected birds. The majority of job seekers are rules followers who will not dare to boycott the recruitment process: even though trap-laden job postings only serve to attract them like moths to a flame who naively believe that companies only hire for the jobs that are advertised online. It's all part and parcel of the corporate recruitment game that keeps job seekers engaged in the recruitment process instead of questioning the process. Just as career sites serve as the bait that attracts you, so too do the job postings. They are the popular dynamic duo mainly used as the conduits of employer branding hocus pocus that razzle-dazzle you into taking that all important next step – filling out the online application.

"There isn't any room for guesswork in applying for jobs online. It's really simple. Follow the instructions in the job posting. Companies think less of (or will ignore) applicants who don't follow the instructions. If the listing says send a cover letter, write one. If the listing says apply online at CareerBuilder, do so." – www.jobdig.com

Is it okay to embellish or fib on your résumé to get an interview? Depends on how you distinguish embellishing from fibbing. The better question to ask is: *Is it okay for companies to fib on their job postings to attract a job seeker?* Little wonder that recruiters have come to rely on the screening tools of applicant tracking systems to compensate for their overly-vague job postings that encourage job seekers to, shall we say, overly-sell their résumés. Recruiters could care less that unqualified job seekers flood the system by applying to jobs for which they do not meet the requirements. Many companies purposely write vague, open-ended job postings to hedge against the risks of accidentally discouraging the right job seekers to apply. This continued practice only creates confusion for all potential applicants as even the unqualified ones will think they have nothing to lose by applying – or embellishing their credentials.

"If we find a good match to Qualcomm requirements and qualifications after you have submitted your résumé, you will be contacted directly by a member of our staffing team. At that time we will be more than happy to discuss your résumé and job interests. While we would like to speak to everyone that has an interest at working at Qualcomm, the volume of résumés does not allow us to perform this courtesy." – Qualcomm

Based on what is written in the job posting, you will need to write your résumé to highlight and showcase why you are the best fit in order to increase your chances of being selected. Recruiters are more interested in laying out the predefined ksa's they believe successful job applicants must possess, rather than allowing job applicants to lay out how their own unique ksa's can meet the challenges of the job. Job postings are static documents that read more like recipes in a cookbook: they give the illusion that anyone can cook if they just follow the instructions and use the listed ingredients. This is employer branding hocus pocus at its finest! Only a small percentage of the people who purchase cookbooks are actually able to make anything worth eating. The same holds true for job postings: only a small percentage of job seekers who attempt to muster up the qualifications listed on job postings will actually capture the attention of a recruiter. The very nature of job postings only serve to force you into modifying your ksa's to fit into a recruiter's definition of the standard corporate employee. In effect, recruiters expect job postings to deliver off-the-shelf "Corporate Employees In A Box".

The hidden message in job postings is that if you do not have a profile matching the recruiter's "copy-paste" requirements, then you must be worthless and unable to contribute any other value. Companies are willing to live with this senseless waste of potential talent because they are purely focused on "hoarding and hiring" the best job applicants. It is the same business practice used in large grocery stores that stock tons of perishable foods. The store managers know that most of the food will be wasted before it is sold, but the bulk prices they pay are cheap, thus allowing them to attract high volumes of shoppers. The costs for recruiters to attract swarms of job seekers with job postings on corporate career sites and external job boards is cheap compared to the value they will gain by attracting the best job applicants. And what is defined as the "best" is purely subjective based on how well your résumé (and other application materials) matches the job postings. Obliging you to try to match the requirements in a job posting to your ksa's is the main trap used by recruiters to weed out the "undesirables".

"The first part of the candidate screening process at McKinsey is a resume review. We use resumes to help us determine whom to invite to our interviewing process. Therefore, it is important for your resume to be the best possible reflection of you and of your achievements." – Mckinsey

The worst transgression reflected in virtually all job postings is the requirement that job applicants meet the minimum number of years of experience as defined arbitrarily by the recruiters and Hiring Managers. **Most large companies are still stuck in the old "seniority rules" model that basically correlates your ability to do a job based on years of work experience.** Despite countless examples of young people who have started major corporations before they even graduated from college, the vast majority of large companies still value seniority over ingenuity. Unfortunately for job seekers, this talent prevention tactic won't be disappearing anytime soon from the job postings sent out by large companies. It should serve as a reminder of the duplicitous nature of job postings and their role in enticing you to apply online. You are not given any contextual information regarding job postings. Recruiters do not reveal any descriptive statistics regarding job postings. You won't see any real-time dashboard information on job postings that tell you at minimum: the number of total applicants, total number of qualified applicants according to the recruiter's specifications, total number of applicants selected for interviews, and total number of hires selected from interviewed candidates.

Many job postings don't give you any transparent details about what to expect from a company's workplace environment, nor do they clearly explain what key performance indicators (kpi's) you will be expected to achieve. If you compare the details you are expected to provide on a résumé versus the details provided on the average job posting, it's clear that recruiters give short shrift to job postings. They are poorly written advertisements that are meant to attract high quality applicants for the recruiter's pleasure. This only serves to stall the career aspirations of job seekers not meeting the ideal candidate requirements. Job seekers are forced to base their decision to apply on these job postings, the oftentimes crummy career sites that host them, and a healthy dose of EBHP. Recruiters demand and expect you to submit a neatly formatted (and appealing) résumé which displays your accomplishments that fit the requirements of the job posting. You will bear the burden of designing the proper résumé format, or worse, paying a professional to write it if you want to increase your chances of being selected. In contrast, there are no universally accepted formats for job postings: they will vary by country, company, and culture. As such, recruiters have no pressure to produce job postings that provide transparent and appealing content.

Even a cursory view of the jobs posted on job boards and corporate career sites suggests that companies show little concern about how the presentation of their job postings reflect upon their image as employers of choice. Consider this listing of just a few of their most egregious breaches of *"Job Posting Etiquette"*:

1. **The Unformatted Job Posting.** Trying to lure job seekers to apply with unflattering, plain-text, run-on sentences is not the best way for a company to present itself. Unformatted text doesn't make for the best read, and is just plain sloppy. Companies correctly invest considerable time and effort in the design and marketing campaigns for products sold to consumers but fail to appreciate how their company's image is adversely affected by unformatted job postings. In the worst case, you are asked to submit an unformatted résumé when applying online; however, you are usually provided the alternative of uploading it in a more appealing, formatted version. First impressions weigh heavily on consumer purchasing decisions just as they do on selection decisions for recruiters. It is unlikely that any recruiter would think highly of a job seeker who sends a plain-text résumé. Companies wouldn't wrap their products in plain-text vanilla packaging and expect them to just fly off the retail shelves, would they? So why is the consumer-orientation different when it pertains to job seekers?

2. **The Two-Page Job Posting.** Recruiters and hiring managers routinely stress the importance of written communication skills and the ability to say more with less. But clearly that only applies to job seekers. Two-page job postings are typically filled with "fluff" and leave job seekers more confused than enlightened. They list every possible duty or task that the job could possibly entail: it's a case of "tell them how the job is to be done" versus "tell them what needs to be done and let them figure out the how". Maybe these companies are anticipating hiring a less-than-desirable job applicant, thus the need to idiot-proof the job postings. They leave nothing to the imagination of the job seeker. These job postings don't convince you that creativity and innovation are valued since apparently the company already knows what needs to be done.

3. **The Half-Page Job Posting.** Too little information is just as bad as too much information. Providing few details of the job duties raises questions about whether the company has thought clearly about the job's value to the organization. Judging by the lack of information in these job postings, that's already answered. These job postings are also marked by liberal use of phrases such as *"duties listed may differ from those actually performed"*, *"other responsibilities as assigned"*, and *"duties listed are not a complete list of all duties to be performed"*. How many job seekers would get away with a half-page résumé? Yet, companies post these half-baked, half-page job postings and expect to attract hordes of qualified job seekers – or repel them. It's debatable whether companies engaging in this practice are really looking to attract qualified job seekers at all: in the case that the job is already secretly filled and the posting is just a cursory activity.

4. **The Mumbo-Jumbo Job Posting.** Some companies believe that their internal company jargon is common language to the outside world. It's clear to job seekers that these companies are also advertising jobs internally to their own employees, but not so clear why no one took the time to edit a version for non-

employees. Besides company jargon, these job postings are replete with dubious job requirements, questionable duties, and open-ended statements that give you few clues on the kpi's for the role. Yet, your résumé would be summarily discarded if it did not list any quantifiable (or qualifying statements) accomplishments for a recruiter to evaluate. A job posting that is confusing, unclear, and vague says more about the company's work environment than it does about the job itself. If there is such confusion in clearly communicating the duties and requirements of a job, then surely there must be communication challenges within the workplace. How many recruiters would give serious consideration to your career focus, professional experience, and job fit if your résumé was a mess of incoherent words and statements?

5. **The Wish-List Job Posting.** Superman is a fictional character; however, some companies create a list of job requirements and qualifications that only a fictional character could possess. Little thought is given to the core qualities needed to perform the job. Even less thought is put into how the desired skills will be utilized in the context of the company's workplace environment. These job postings only focus on the company's profile of the ideal candidate. This is the equivalent of your using that now-antiquated "Objective" heading on a résumé to state your ideal job duties. While there is nothing inherently wrong with a company's desire to hire the right person for a job, it is probably fair to say that making a wish-list won't necessarily accomplish the task. Some of these job postings reflect a company's lack of strategy regarding the job's role within the department and organization. Others are written so precisely to attract only the ideal applicants that they mistakenly screen out many of the right ones. There are even those that are purposely written to discourage you from applying. Why? Because the company has already decided its hiring selection and merely posts these jobs in compliance with HR policies.

Job seekers are left with no other choice but to decipher these mangled job postings and attempt to fit themselves neatly into their requirements. Based on my research of over 100 globally-ranked employers, a large majority have no mechanism that allows you to communicate by phone or live chat to ask questions about the job postings before you apply. There are no recruiter hot lines or personal emails provided for you at this stage in the recruitment process. What you see is what you get, and it will be your responsibility to match your skills against an oftentimes ambiguous job posting. So who really benefits from job postings? Certainly, not you! You will be burdened with trying to pick out the essential job requirements from an oftentimes poorly-written document. While you are jumping through hoops trying to make sense of the job posting, there are at least a few dozen job seekers doing the same. You alone will bear the burden of creating a coherent résumé – along with any other information requested in the online application – to satisfy vague job posting requirements.

Chapter 11
Applicant Tracking Systems: Anti-Talent Systems In Disguise

"The BMW Group prefers online applications. These are the only ones that can be effectively processed – and stored searchably. All points to be observed when submitting such an application can be found in this section of the career pages." – BMW

After you search the job postings hosted on the corporate career site, you will be directed to complete an online job application through the Applicant Tracking Systems (ATS). The ATS will collect various amounts of detailed information regarding your personal and professional profile. In the best case, it will simply pull the basic details from your uploaded résumé, allow you to upload additional documents, and complete optional surveys before submitting the application. In the worst case, it will require you to complete pre-screening questions, input additional details not found on the résumé (like contact information for prior supervisors and references, salary history, desired salary), and in some cases, write a short essay. ATS's are an unavoidable part of the corporate recruitment process. They are essential to capturing, storing, and transforming job applicants into bits of uploaded data. Recruiters are then able to harvest this data, rank-order it, and judge the worthiness of your candidacy without ever having to actually see your application. Yet, you will be instructed to submit an excellent application if you want to convince the recruiters of your candidacy. There won't be any exceptions made for you to meet directly with a Hiring Manager. Regardless if you are an experienced professional or a recent college graduate, you will have to search the job postings database and complete an online application.

Most businesses understand the importance of segmenting their customer base in order to provide services to meet their unique needs. In the airline industry, there are separate check-in lines for economy class customers and business class customers. In supermarkets, there are separate check-out lines for bulk purchases and for small purchases. The fact that all job seekers applying online are treated the same does not seem to follow sound business practices. When applying online, your fate is left in the hands of a software program that will rank and file you according to how well your application matches requirements set by the recruiter. However, it is unlikely that the ATS is 100% reliable when it comes to selecting the right talent. Most corporate recruiters are not going to look at every application for every job posting they are managing: especially for high-volume jobs, or high-paying jobs that attract a lot of applicants. Instead, these **recruiters rely on the ATS to do the dirty work for them and rank order the applications from best match to worst match – thus, allowing the recruiter to review only the top matches.** This is good for the recruiter but bad for the talented job seekers who might be mistakenly screened out.

"All applications must be made via our Careers website. This ensures that your CV is forwarded to the relevant recruiter and your application is managed effectively." – Nokia

There is no honor in applying online. Doing so puts you into a small pond with other job applicants to be speared like a helpless fish by big game hunting recruiters. The ATS is unfeeling and acts without emotion. It cannot interpret your passion nor predict how you will perform as an employee. It only sees binary code and breaks you down into bits and bytes that can be numerically quantified, compared, and ranked. If it does not calculate that you warrant a high ranking among the other applicants vying for the same job, it will place you in the middle of the pack – or worse, the bottom quartile. The ATS is the ultimate tool in the recruiter's arsenal to find the best and the brightest job applicants. Regardless of what value you can bring to a company, it will not matter if you cannot convince the ATS. You won't even be given the courtesy of speaking to a live person if the software bots scrubbing the applicant database do not deem you worthy. Indeed, you will be categorized, tagged, and quarantined like a rabid dog. For the prideful and genteel job applicant, there is no greater shame than to be rejected in such a defiled manner.

Too many job applicants want desperately to believe that some recruiter is actually taking the time to find a job for them. Maybe that is easier to believe than actually facing the fact that you have just converted yourself into a faceless number through the ATS with little hope of ever being contacted. It is probably accurate to say that the vast majority of job seekers don't enjoy completing online applications. And why should they? Recruiters oblige them to fill out online fields of redundant information with no promise of an interview or timely feedback on their application status. It is indeed a flawed system for the job seekers, but accomplishes its intended purpose for the recruiters. There is no shortage of literature and advice on how to game the ATS by loading your résumé, cover letter, and other materials with key words found in the job posting and associated industry. Therefore, recruiters don't always get the desired candidate, but instead, the desired application. Applicant Tracking Systems reward the best application writers – not necessarily the best applicants. Talk about search engine optimization (SEO) gone bad!

"We search our résumé database regularly and then contact the people we'd like to learn more about. Unfortunately, we're not able to make personal contact with people who are not going to be invited in for interviews, but we keep all résumés on file for several months." – Amazon

The ATS controls what you can submit (and not submit) in support of your case to be selected for further review. Your entire application will be at the mercy of the screening criteria set by the recruiter. The standard traditional résumé and cover letter form the core of your application and most screening criteria will be based on their contents. Job seekers who write the best résumés and cover letters (or have a paid professional do it) greatly increase their chances of bypassing the initial ATS screens. In this regard, **Applicant Tracking Systems tend to behave more like Anti-Talent Systems** because they keep out many potential employees who don't submit SEO-powered applications. If you have not had success using online applications, you are unlikely to apply to the same companies multiple times – even if you have the best profile for an advertised job. What incentive would you have to apply over and over again to the same company? Clearly if they were too boneheaded to not be able to see how you could be of value to them in other positions, then it is unlikely they'll view your future applications any different. In the end, only one person will be hired per job posting no matter how many job seekers apply to a job, are interviewed, or short listed. Don't expect corporate recruiters to lend a helping hand if you are not selected.

All ATS's serve the same purpose; however, there are some that facilitate the process better than others. It is worth giving an overview of the types of systems you will encounter whether your job search is national or international. A company won't win any awards for having the best ATS but the type of system it uses can give you clues about its recruiters' customer orientation – with you being the customer. It's fair to say if a company's HR department cannot design an ATS that is job seeker-oriented, then that will not bode well for that HR department's service-orientation towards employees.

1. **The Single-Country Applicant Tracking System.** This system is good for companies that operate in one country but bad when companies replicate this model to other countries in which they operate. Companies with decentralized operations are prone to using this type of ATS. It is not uncommon for each country where a company operates to have its own proprietary ATS, thereby obliging job seekers looking for multi-country opportunities to repeat the application process several times. Depending on the cultural diversity of the country, these systems may also offer the option to register and search for jobs in multiple languages (whether or not those languages are official languages of the country). An example is the case of an ATS in the United States offering registration and job search in both English and Spanish – even though Spanish is not an official language of the United States. A second example is the case of an ATS in Spain offering

registration and job search in Spanish, Catalán, Galician, and Basque – all recognized languages of Spain.

2. **The Regional Applicant Tracking System.** This system is convenient for job seekers applying within a certain region like North America, Asia-Pacific, or Latin America where companies have geographic operations. Thus, you don't have to register in separate ATS's for different countries of interest within the designated regions. These systems will allow you to register in only one language that is designated by the ATS and will display jobs in that language only. In the cases where English is not the language, these systems might still include jobs written in English since it is the recognized global business language; but this will be only for the jobs requiring fluency in English. Regional systems are similar to Single-Country systems with the exception of including more than one country. An example is the case of a job seeker using a regional system to search for jobs in various Latin American countries. Even though there a several official languages in Latin America, this system only allows you to search job postings written in the one language designated by the company which could be Spanish, Portuguese, French, or English.

3. **The Single-Language|Multinational Applicant Tracking System.** This system lists jobs in only one language for various countries or regions, thereby allowing job seekers a convenient and centralized search. It is more beneficial to job seekers who are fluent in the designated language (usually the language where the company is based) as it allows them to search for local, national, and international jobs from one site. Job seekers who do not possess the required language fluency will be excluded from this system by the natural language barrier. These systems are centralized at the corporate headquarters and are generally used to recruit for professional jobs that will require fluency in the language used by the company to conduct its multinational business (usually English). For example, a company based in the USA will allow job seekers

to look for job postings in English in every country where the company operates.

4. **The Multi-Language|Multinational Applicant Tracking System.** This system lists jobs in multiple languages for various countries or regions, and facilitates a convenient and centralized way to search. It reduces application barriers by allowing you to register in several official languages designated by the company, as well as search for jobs posted in those languages. The languages offered will be limited to what the recruiters make available for the designated countries or regions. These systems are composed of three types: 1) the system that offers multiple language registrations for the ATS, multi-national job searches, and jobs posted in multiple languages (you are unable to filter the job postings by language – only by country); 2) the system that offers multi-national job searches with jobs posted in multiple languages (you are unable to filter the job postings by language – only by country); and 3) the system that offers multi-national job searches with the ability to select the languages you want the job postings listed in. These ATS's usually require separate registrations to access different countries or regions according to how the company is geographically segmented. Even though these systems can allow job seekers to choose from multiple language options, they are not considered global since their scale and scope are limited by the company's size. The number of languages listed in the system will be limited to only a few per region. For example, the EMEA region (Europe, Middle East & Africa) might only allow registration and job searching in English, German, French, Spanish, and Italian – thus representing only a small percentage of the official languages in the region.

5. **The Global Applicant Tracking System.** This is the most efficient and client-friendly system because it allows job seekers to create only one profile and search jobs in all countries or regions where the company operates. Only a global company will have the capacity to have this ATS. These

systems also allow you to register in your native language, or even search for job descriptions written in your native language (if the language is a major world language) and other languages within your fluency. This is especially useful for job seekers possessing multiple work authorizations or who speak multiple languages. For example, a job seeker can register in any of the languages provided by the ATS and still be allowed to view all the jobs posted in the system regardless of the language in which they are written. With the global system, all job seeker actions take place on one ATS. The system is usually centralized which allows all recruiters, regardless of geographic location, to access the same database in order to source talent. Even though the odds of your being randomly contacted by a recruiter who is actively searching the database for a particular profile is small, it at least allows for the possibility.

6. **The Social Media-Enhanced Applicant Tracking System.** This system can have any of the characteristics of the aforementioned types. It usually has a function that allows you to use the data from your LinkedIn profile to complete part of the application. It also shows you the current employees (and former) in your networks who are currently working at the company. However, it is debatable how useful this feature is to job seekers since it does more to speed up the application process, than it does to improve your chances of getting selected. The whole intent of using social media networks is to bypass the ATS altogether in order to obtain an interview directly with a recruiter or Hiring Manager. Furthermore, you can easily go onto LinkedIn prior to applying for a job in order to find out if anyone in your network has any current or former ties to employees at your target companies. Still, these systems are at least a small step in the right direction towards fully engaging job seekers in two-way communication via social media technologies before applying online.

All Applicant Tracking Systems generally follow the same information collection protocol: 1) Registration; 2) Résumé and Cover Letter Upload; 3) Profile Information and Source Tracking; 4) Work Experience; 5) Education; 6) Screening Questions (optional); 7) Additional Information Upload (optional); 8) Voluntary Information Survey (optional); and 9) Verification and Confirmation. Depending on the parameters of the ATS set by the recruiter, the online application process can take anywhere between one and three hours to complete. That includes the time it takes to customize your application documents but it does not include the immeasurable time you might spend researching the company's business and EVP. What incentive do you have to complete an online application? Absolutely none! All of the time and effort you will spend completing the application comes with no guarantee of receiving an interview – let alone receiving a response from a real person. The more likely guarantee of what you can look forward to receiving is an email confirming receipt of your application, followed shortly after by an automated rejection email – provided the company is courteous enough to communicate your status.

"All openings for this position have either been filled or cancelled. Thank you for your interest in employment opportunities with GE and for your patience in awaiting a response.

There are still many opportunities at GE – we post positions daily. If you would like to learn about other available positions, please visit GE Careers. To track positions that might interest you, log into GE Careers, click Search Agent Manager and follow the instructions. You will then be notified by email when job openings that meet your search criteria are posted.

We wish you every success in your next career move.

Sincerely,

GE Human Resources

*PLEASE NOTE: This is an unmonitored mailbox. Please do not reply to this email."

Chapter 12
Psychometric Testing: Quantifying The Standard Corporate Employee

"If your application passes screening, you'll be invited to take a couple of online aptitude tests which assess your logical and numerical reasoning." – Unilever

Psychometric tests attempt to measure attributes like intelligence, aptitude, and personality that a company deems are necessary for an employee to be successful. Their purpose is to provide a company with insight into how you might work with other people, handle job-related stress, and cope with the intellectual demands of the job. Any company that makes psychometric testing a part of its recruitment process is not trying to filter in talent, but rather, screen out "mentally-impaired" applicants. That may be an exaggeration, but **if these tests are so valid then every professional employee in the organization would take them – and that does not happen.** The fact that a company even uses psychometric testing during the recruitment process says more about the company than it does about the job seekers who take the test. In search of excellence, many global companies rely on standardized testing to find competent corporate employees. These tests are a boon to the incompetent recruiters who use them to hide their own inability to properly assess the competency of job applicants through more creative means.

"P&G uses online assessments to measure skills and accomplishments that generally do not emerge from interviews. These assessments are critical as they help determine if it is equally beneficial for you to continue through the hiring process." – Procter & Gamble

Only certain jobs will require psychometric testing: those deemed by the company as requiring the extra seal of approval these tests purportedly provide. You have to ask yourself if it is worth it to apply to a job if your fate can be decided by the results of a standardized test. Yet, this is an obstacle that job seekers have to plan for when going through the throes of the formal recruitment process. Once again, instead of focusing on how you can best contribute to the company's bottom line, recruiters are more concerned with making sure you do not test in the bottom quartile. I guess your work ethic, ability to innovate, and passion for the job are just not that important if they cannot be statistically measured through multiple choice testing. These tests cannot measure the qualities that are found in the truly successful employees: for example, they are unable to assess the influence you will have on the performance of co-workers or the value you will bring to a job. Yet, you will be sorted and categorized by your test results before you even get a chance to show how you can impact business results.

Recruiters will state that these tests are only one part of the recruitment process and are not used exclusively in the decision-making process, but this is not always true. Some companies use psychometric tests during the pre-interview phase to decide which job seekers warrant an interview request. Other companies use the tests following the application submission to determine who will go further in the process. Either way, companies which rely on these tests to make interviewing or hiring decisions do so in the name of the standardized corporate employee. This is the employee who falls within the bell curve of recruitment specifications. Unfortunately, you are not given an option to see the psychometric profile of the standard corporate employee – or at least those of your potential co-workers. If that option was available, then at least you would be able to see what types of psychometric profiles are valued throughout the company and make a decision on whether it is in your best interest to apply.

"We use online psychometric tests to help filter our application numbers, and many candidates do not meet the benchmark at this stage. This is therefore a key part of the process – there is no point showing us that you have the skills and capabilities that we're looking for in your application form only to be let down by the tests." – HSBC

Many companies express their embrace of diversity and inclusion in terms of thought, personality, and aptitude but it is difficult to understand how the use of these tests support that embrace. The very nature of these tests normalizes everyone according to a predetermined sample population. Therefore, companies are looking for "replicates" of their standard corporate employees versus assessing people who offer contrasting views and abilities. Job seekers want to be valued for who they are and what they bring to the company – not for how their psychometric profiles measure against a bell curve. It is largely the fear of hiring the wrong job seeker that drives companies to use these tests. This is flawed thinking and has more to do with the values and mindset of the company, than with the job seekers themselves. **What companies believe they are unable to evaluate through observations and interviews, they will rely on these surrogate tests to do it for them.**

You should beware the companies that make psychometric testing a part of the online application. Those are the ones that won't even speak to you if your scores fall outside the "norm". Since you won't know what the "norm" is, it's best to not even take the test. This is one of those "tells" in the game where you have to ask yourself: *How does this aid me?* Recruiters don't give you any statistics on the profiles of the employees who took the test versus the ones who didn't. These tests are only valid if they show a clear distinction in the performance of those who score within the norm versus those who don't. Curiously, information on their validity is not made public by the companies using them. Recruiters use many types of psychometric tests and the particular test used during a recruitment process will vary by company, industry, and job. There is continued debate around the validity of these tests but that is not going to stop their increased usage. That being said, these tests seem to be a reflection of the lack of trust recruiters (and even some Hiring Managers) have in job applicants rather than the supposed accuracy they provide in selecting the best job candidates. Many job seekers can expect to take the same *"Standard Corporate Employee Tests"* at some point in the formal recruitment process.

1. **The Personality Assessment Test.** Your personality may help or hinder you in certain jobs, or certain workplace environments. While it is possible for you to adapt your personality as needed for a particular job, companies using this test won't take that into consideration while you're still a job applicant. Knowledge of yourself is always a good thing and allows you to make proper decisions regarding your job search. Unfortunately for you, companies will use these test results to either place you in the job they think is the best fit for you given your personality profile, or reject you from the recruitment process altogether.

2. **The Verbal Reasoning Test.** You won't have any problems with this test if you are great at analyzing written statements and following instructions. These tests evaluate your communication skills as well as critical thinking skills. And you thought your college degrees already certified that – think again! A college degree isn't what it used to be, so companies will use their own certification to ensure that you have the desired verbal reasoning skills.

3. **The Numerical Reasoning Test.** If you are not great at analyzing data from spreadsheets or tables, then you probably need to excuse yourself from the recruitment process. Like all timed tests, they are more concerned with your ability to spot trends and patterns quickly. Even though you might be good with numbers when given enough time, these tests don't take that into consideration – and neither will the recruiter.

4. **The Emotional Intelligence Test.** The important qualities that companies value are how well you manage yourself, your relationship with others, and your reaction to events outside your control. This test will evaluate your emotional intelligence based on your self-management and social-management skills. These companies want to predict the likelihood that you will be successful during the good times, the bad times, and the ugly times. They also want to put the onus on you to endure their dysfunctional workplace

environments: it's much cheaper to hire punching bag employees than to improve workplace policies and practices.

Companies justify subjecting job seekers to these mental dissection tests, and then punishing or rewarding them based on the results. It gives them another so-called objective metric to compare against your interview results and other application submissions. Regardless of your university grades, excellence at problem solving, past professional performance, or proven leadership; you will still be measured against the results of your psychometric tests. You have a 50/50 chance to score well based on the company's definition of "well". You will be lucky if the company gives you any useful hints or tips in preparing for the tests: or ANY preparation time for that matter. Companies will not tell you how much weight they give to the results of psychometric tests nor are they obliged to share the test results. You may feel pressure to try to game the system by giving the answers you believe most represent what the company desires. You might even try to change or modify your natural profile to be more aligned with an expected ideal. But in the end, you'll be the only loser in this game. How long do you think you can get away with trying to be someone you're not? It didn't work for *The Talented Mr. Ripley* – and it won't for you either.

Chapter 13
Interviews: Interrogations Versus Discussions

"If you meet our benchmark in the online tests, we will invite you to have a telephone interview. We conduct interviews by phone because we receive applications from all over the world and attending a face-to-face meeting at this stage can be impractical for many candidates." – HSBC

Interviews are an extremely important part of the recruitment process, and job seekers should look forward to having them. It is an opportunity for you to evaluate a company's employees and its values. Your objective should be to look for the companies that offer the best workplace environment where you can maximize your contributions and skills. The interview is not just about the company asking you 20 questions about your past performance and why you want to work for them: it is also the time for you to investigate pertinent details of the company's EVP that could either aid or hinder your success. Therefore, it is important for you to prepare your own list of pertinent questions regarding your fit with the company. Ask thoughtful and penetrating questions that allow you to assess the business acumen of the interviewer as well as gather some details about the company not found through your research: *"What do you consider to be your firm's most important assets?"*; *"What are the performance expectations of this position over the first 12 months?"*; *"What is the overall structure of the company and how does your department fit the structure?"*; and *"What happened to the last person who held this job?"* When you make it past the Applicant Tracking System and Psychometric Tests, then you must take advantage of the opportunity you will finally be afforded to speak with a live person.

"It is 3M policy not to give contact information to external applicants. If, after you apply, it is determined that your skills and abilities match our hiring needs, you will be contacted directly for an interview." – 3M

Unfortunately for you, this live person probably won't be the person for whom you would be working – it will be a recruiter. Your first challenge will be to convince the recruiter you are worthy to speak with the real decision makers in the recruitment process. Failure to do so will result in a quick rejection from further consideration. Recruiters are like Agent Smith in *The Matrix*: they are guarding all the doors and holding all the keys. A lot of recruiters cherish their role as company gatekeepers and purported caretakers of talent selection. They are more concerned with asking job candidates questions that will screen them out, instead of questions that will filter in the ones best suited to deliver value to the company. Getting past them will not be easy and they will fight fiercely to protect the corporation from being infested by unworthy job candidates. Do not expect any sympathy or any help completing your responses to the probing questions that will be lobbed at you. Corporate recruiters will only show favor to the job candidates prepared to play the game: the ones who will dutifully structure their responses using the STAR technique (situation or task, action, result) or any of its interview strategy variants.

Interviews tend to be conducted by companies as a one-way affair: recruiters and Hiring Managers ask all the questions and you are expected to answer them to their full satisfaction. Recruiters may encourage you to ask questions, but most are largely incapable of answering any questions of substance. **Therefore, interviews don't follow the path of a mutually beneficial discussion, but rather, the path of an interrogation.** The thinking by companies is that since they are the ones who will pay the salaries and benefits, then they have the most to lose from a hiring mistake. These interviewers will pester you with all types of questions that oblige you to explain in explicit detail your past, present, and future. Most job candidates will find themselves on the defensive more often than not, and scrambling to regurgitate responses they think present them as the "employee of choice". And just when you think you have passed one interview hurdle, you will have to repeat the process again and again with several more interviewers who will oftentimes ask you the same questions.

"We use behavioral-based interviews to get to know you. The real you. What makes you tick? What have you accomplished so far? To do this we'll ask questions about previous accomplishments or how you've handled situations in the past. This is also your opportunity to find out about us. We believe two-way communication starts from day one, so ask away." – Procter & Gamble

Interviewers will ask you a combination of behavioral-based questions to quantify and qualify your personal behavior and professional skills. While they are measuring your responses according to a rating scale, you will be left to wonder if you have given the "acceptable" answers. Most of the questions you will be asked will have very little to do with your ability to meet the challenges listed in the job posting. *"Can you give me an example of your teamwork skills?"* Before answering this question, you should find out how the recruiter defines "teamwork" and "skills" because oftentimes what they really want to know is your individual contribution that added value to the team. If what you consider value-adding differs from the recruiter's expectations, then you might be given a low rating. Throughout the interview process, you will find yourself tripping and stumbling over questions that can be interpreted in various ways. *"Can you give me an example of your leadership skills?"* This seems like an innocuous question until you realize that what you and the interviewer consider leadership can be entirely different. If you haven't mastered the recommended techniques for answering behavioral interview questions, the interviewers will quickly remove you from further consideration.

Instead of concentrating on how to add value to the company prior to a scheduled interview, job candidates are baited into preparing answers for standard interview questions. This should be your first clue to the nature of the recruiter's intentions. If they want to evaluate whether or not you can do a particular job, then there are better methods to determine that. Yet, recruiters are more than happy to keep up appearances in the game by showing favor to the job candidates who provide the best answers. Unless the recruiter is really competent and knows how to properly evaluate talent, most job candidates who don't respond to behavior-based interview questions with a structured answer will be given short shrift. If you are competent in function but not competent in form when answering interview questions – you lose! You can be knocked out of the game early if you fail to answer properly even the most standard of interview questions that have nothing to do with job skills, such as: 1) *What are your salary expectations?*; 2) *Why did you leave your last job?*; and 3) *How long will you stay with our company?*

Non-Standard Interview Questions

Every now and then job seekers will encounter a new breed of corporate recruiters that dare to be different with their interview questions. However, being different with interview questions does not equate to being effective. If you are interviewed by some of today's tech giants, it is a given that you will be asked questions reminiscent of a blue sky case interview (how many red gumballs are in a gumball machine?). Corporate recruiters at Google have asked job candidates the following questions (www.online.wsj.com): 1) *A book has N pages, numbered the usual way, from 1 to N. The total number of digits in the page numbers is 1,095. How many pages does the book have?*; 2) *"A man pushed his car to a hotel and lost his fortune. What happened?"* How any company can justify these "brain-teaser" questions as valid in determining a job candidate's ability to perform is inexplicable. However, it's a growing trend that more and more recruiters are adopting. Unscrupulous recruiters spring these loaded questions upon unwitting job seekers with the justification that these questions can accurately measure how a potential employee will impact the business. Recruiters and Hiring Managers engaged in this practice have convinced themselves that the job candidates who can answer these questions are better than the ones who can't.

The use of standard interview questions is good for the interviewers to compare multiple job candidates against each other but bad for the candidates who are trying to differentiate themselves. Once in a while, you will have an unstructured interview that resembles an actual discussion. During these rare occasions, you can be more relaxed and not rely on scripted responses to standard interview questions. Discussions give both you and the interviewer an opportunity to speak about the specifics of the job and how you are uniquely able to take on the challenges. Oftentimes a discussion can lead to you and the interviewer finding an entirely different job other than what was originally available; or it can lead to either of you realizing that the job is just not a good match. However, recruiters are not interested in discussions; they are interested in interrogations that put you on the hot seat like a hostile witness. Even with situational interviews and case interviews, you are being measured based on controlled (and oftentimes unrealistic) data that is expected to validate your fit with the job and workplace environment. Nevertheless, virtually every job candidate will have to pass through the *"Golden Troika Of Spanish Inquisitions"* before gaining access to the next stage in the corporate recruitment process.

1. **Phone Screen Interview.** Before you get all excited about being selected for a phone interview, you are well-advised to remember that it is not for your benefit. At this stage, recruiters only care about your salary history, current salary, and expected salary. Job candidates who say the wrong number will be politely excused from further consideration. Some companies may round out the phone interview with harmless questions about your willingness to relocate or clarification of some details on your résumé. But your answers to the salary questions are the real meat and potatoes of this interview.

2. **Videoconference Interview.** Whether or not you receive this interview will depend on the recruiter's preference. It's an intermediate step to allow the recruiter an opportunity to interview you in a virtual medium that allows for visual observation. This allows the recruiter an inexpensive way to screen you and decide if you warrant advancement in the recruitment process. Job candidates might receive a typical behavioral interview at this point, or get asked some straight-

forward questions about their interest and motivation to work for the company. The recruiter wants to make sure that you fit the image of the company by observing your professional appearance and composure. So if you have any bad habits like biting your nails when you get nervous or giggling like a child when you get flustered, then expect this interview to be the last contact you'll have with the company.

3. **Onsite Interview.** Here is where the so-called "real interviews" take place and they can include behavioral interviews, case interviews, situational interviews, panel interviews, or a combination of them all. You can spend from a half-day to a full-day conducting interviews with various stakeholders in the recruitment process such as the recruiter, the Hiring Manager, and potential co-workers. A job candidate's success at this stage will be a combination of many factors that include his personal fit within the organization, his professional value proposition, and his ability to answer "correctly" a barrage of interrogatories. Expect questions more focused on why you left your last job, why you want to leave your current one, or why you've changed jobs twice in the past three years, rather than any meaningful questions about how your prior experience will benefit the company. Expect questions about your handling of hypothetical situations instead of any discussion of how you would be an asset to the company. However, when all is said and done, the person you will need to convince the most is the Hiring Manager. That is the one person who has the final word on your candidacy.

Job candidates will have to successfully pass through all of the interview stages in order to stay in the rat race. This can sometimes feel like you are in an obstacle course with each obstacle becoming more challenging than the last. Even your success during the various interview stages won't guarantee that you will receive a job offer. Remember, you are in competition with other job candidates who might be just as prepared and qualified for the same job. Interviews are conducted for the interviewer's pleasure – not yours. The interviewing team will have the luxury of carefully reviewing all of the interviewed candidates and selecting the ones they want to advance. Interviews are highly subjective and your rating will depend on how your responses resonate with the expectations of the interviewer. How do you benefit from traditional interviews? You don't! They are designed for the interviewer to evaluate your fit, not the other way around. You'll be lucky if you're able to get past the initial interviews given by the incompetent recruiters. Most companies will decide whether or not you'll be extended an employment offer after a maximum of three interview rounds. If this is not the case, then you will be sent to an additional stage in the recruitment process.

Chapter 14
Assessment Centers: The Rejection Centers

"There is nothing that you can do to prepare in advance for the Final Selection Center (FSC), other than to relax and be yourself. This is our opportunity to see how you perform in a number of different situations, against clearly defined criteria. We also want to get to know you better and understand what drives you towards a career as an International Manager." – HSBC

Job candidates who are invited to an Assessment Center (AC) will be evaluated, poked, and prodded like thoroughbred racehorses being assessed by potential buyers. At the AC, you will be lined up along with all of the other candidates who are competing for the same jobs. It is the ultimate battle to the death for the ultimate prize that would make even the fiercest gladiator proud! Because the AC is usually the final stage in the recruitment process, it is your final opportunity to present your wares and show the "right stuff" in an array of activities designed by the assessors. These centers can also be where the psychometric tests are taken if they were not administered at an earlier stage. Either way, the objective of these centers is to "normalize" candidates against predefined job profiles in order to identify those who fall neatly within the boundaries of the bell curve – and to reject the outliers (in the bottom quartile, of course). In reality, these centers are only useful to further evaluate the potential "replicates" of the standardized employee mold.

"An Assessment Center consists of a standardized evaluation of behavior based on multiple evaluations including: job-related simulations, interviews, and/or psychological tests. Job Simulations are used to evaluate candidates on behaviors relevant to the most critical aspects (or competencies) of the job." – www.hr-guide.com

Some job candidates will naturally fit the desired mold. Others will either attempt to twist, fold, and contort themselves into the corporate box that they believe the company is seeking to fill; or they will try to be their natural selves and hope for the best.

The candidates who have researched the company's culture in detail and determined the success factors they need to demonstrate during the assessment activities will have the most success at "gaming" the system. In reality, Assessment Centers are no different than Applicant Tracking Systems. The former screens you out in person for not displaying the ideal aptitude and attitude, while the latter screens you out online for not submitting the ideal résumé and profile. What is peculiar throughout all this Assessment Center madness (as with the Psychometric Tests) is the fact that the majority of these companies purport to value diversity and inclusion – but clearly only within the parameters of the bell curve. In this respect, Assessment Centers behave more like Rejection Centers: only they probably reject more candidates who can't play the game well, instead of the truly unsuitable ones.

How does the AC aid your job candidacy? It doesn't, really. Unless you enjoy feeling like a lab rat trying to find the exit in a complex maze, it is safe to assume that the AC will not be an evaluation in which you look forward to participate. Of course, recruiters will excitedly inform you of your selection to attend an AC day as if it is a badge of honor. Indeed, you will be made to feel special to be part of an elite group of job candidates vying for the ultimate prize – an employment offer. This is the magic of employer branding hocus pocus! Only supernatural marketing can transform a lab experiment into a buzz-worthy, invitation-only assessment center. Do not be deceived by the semantics. As Shakespeare said, *"A rose by any other name would smell as sweet."* Only the AC is no rose, nor does it smell like one. It stinks from here to high heaven! The AC is the ultimate dog and pony show where you will be expected to jump over hurdles and trot around like a cuddly poodle. **Recruiters and Hiring Managers would be better served by letting the invited job candidates spend the day working with their prospective co-workers, than by subjecting them to contrived simulations that do not add any business value.**

Assessment Centers have devolved into Medieval Fairs. In ancient times, seafaring merchants traversed the globe to procure the fine wines, luxurious materials, and exotic animals that would fetch the most value in the market place. They would then put these goods on open display for wealthy buyers to inspect, select, and purchase for their own personal needs. Nowadays, the seafarer is the corporate recruiter who perpetually searches the globe for high-potential employees and the wealthy buyers are the Hiring Managers desiring to stock their shelves with the best talent. Regardless of your unique potential, the AC is a talent showcase where selected job candidates are expected to shake their tail feathers like a peacock and garner the most votes. It is a sham in which you will be obliged to participate if you want to win the prize. Otherwise, you will be left in the animal shelter like an abandoned dog that nobody wants to adopt. Assessors will be watching you closely while grading your personal and professional skillset in a standardized setting. Just like a controlled lab experiment, these assessors will grade job candidates strictly against the ideal criteria they have predefined. Thus, there will not be much room for error and there will be no prizes for runner-ups.

"Our assessment centers are designed so that we can observe you taking part in a number of activities to assess the competencies we believe are important for our business. These will vary depending on which role you have applied for, however you can expect to take part in further group activities, interviews and case studies." – IBM

You won't get a second chance to make a first impression during observed exercises and activities. It is of no concern to the company if you are having a bad day or not feeling your best. The AC is meant to predict how you will behave under a given set of circumstances and won't always take into account your ability to adapt to a situation or to learn from a mistake. The main goal is to evaluate all candidates in the same way, rate and rank order them, and make hiring decisions based on the assessors' analysis. While some companies might fool you into believing that the AC is for your benefit and will be used to find the best fit for you within the company, the reality is that it is often used to find "corporate ready" employees who will require little to no training in the behaviors and skills desired by the company. Not all AC's are the same and they vary in form and content as much as the companies that use them. Candidates who have the (mis)fortune of being invited to an AC can breathe a sigh of relief at being one step away from the end of the formal recruitment process. However, before celebrating another milestone, candidates will have to pass through the AC's *"Five Trials Of Wisdom"*.

1. **The In-Tray Exercise.** What you will find in this exercise is purely up to the assessors. Its main purpose is to see how well you organize, prioritize, and extract information from data in a given set of documents in a set time period. Talk about a lab rat experiment! Job candidates who don't work well under pressure will probably be the sacrificial lambs at this stage.

2. **The Presentation Exercise.** It is highly unlikely for you to reach the Assessment Center without having demonstrated good communication skills. The point of this exercise is to see how well you deliver a message to a group on a topic chosen by either the assessors or you. Job candidates who don't like to speak in front of groups, or have trouble putting together a coherent presentation in a short time period, will not look forward to this exercise.

3. **The Group Exercise.** This is the "Can you play well with others?" exercise. It's no different than observing a group of kids on a playground and noting which kids have been properly home trained. Here, assessors will be observing how well candidates work together and the specific characteristics they display. One could fairly call this exercise Emotional Intelligence 101 because your social skills will be on full display. This exercise won't bode well for the job candidates who were childhood bullies or didn't like to share their toys.

4. **The Panel Interview.** Once again you have to return to the interrogation style of interviews: except this time, it will be done by managers and trained assessors. They are more likely to ask tougher questions than were asked during prior interviews and will be observing how you handle yourself

during a pressure-filled interrogation. The trick here is to maintain your composure and attempt to connect with each interviewer. Job candidates who are practiced in yoga will do just fine in this interview. Those who are on edge, or easily stressed out, might just crash and burn.

5. **The Role Play Exercise.** Job candidates have to remember that this exercise is not about what they would like to do, but rather, what the company expects them to do. You might be asked to assume a role that has to deal with a conflict involving the role assumed by an assessor (who might play an indignant client or an under-performing subordinate). This exercise can probably be labeled as Emotional Intelligence 102 because you will be evaluated on your ability to perceive, use, understand, and manage your emotions along with those of others when dealing with the role of the assessor. Any violent outbursts during this exercise will ensure the end of your candidacy.

"Will you pass your assessment centre? Learn from the assessors themselves how assessment centres work and what candidates need to do in order to perform well. Real assessors walk you through the most common exercises and explain what they look for." – www.assessmentday.co.uk

The corporate recruitment game is designed to find the "company man" and "company woman". The AC is the final defense the game has to screen out unsuitable candidates who slipped by the recruitment gatekeepers. It is not always the best candidate who does well at these Assessment Centers, but rather, the candidate who plays the game the best. For each assessment exercise there is a strategy for completing it successfully. Assessors and company managers have become accustomed to selecting the candidates who are smart enough to pass the day-long trials and tribulations presented at the AC. Candidates who are unable to meet the standards of the AC exercises risk being outliers, and thus, rejected from the process. At this stage of the recruitment process, companies are not looking for creative and innovative people who think outside the box. Instead, they are looking to screen out the candidates who do not meet the standard criteria set by AC assessors. In order to be selected from the AC and emerge as a winner, you have to play the role of the standard corporate employee. If you are unwilling to play this role, it is better for you to exclude yourself from the recruitment process at this stage, because sooner or later, the company will do it for you.

Chapter 15
Employment Offer: Low Cost Versus High Value

"Once you will have completed the interview process, and if your application leads to a consensus of all the people you have met, the Human Resources Director will make you a contractual hiring offer." – Loreal

Job candidates who have been made an employment offer can be happy that they have successfully made it to the last stage of the recruitment process. This is why you enter the recruitment process and endure so many arduous trials. You now feel like a battle-tested warrior. But nothing is ever as simple as it seems. Depending on your skills, unique value proposition, and how the company values them; you may receive a standard employment offer that is better than expected, worse than expected, or somewhere in between. The recruiter will usually attempt to make you an offer that puts you on a pay scale with other employees at your perceived level. Unfortunately for you, companies determine your pay range based on factors that have nothing to do with the value you can generate for them. Potential employees will be grouped together according to the level and type of education obtained, years of professional experience (including internships and co-ops in the case of students), test scores, and prior salary history.

Of course, this doesn't fairly value your unique value proposition – assuming you have one. Since many companies have no accurate way to value the compensation for their jobs, they rely on you to do it for them. That's why recruiters ask you on the job application and during the initial phone screen interview to tell your salary history, current salary, or expected salary. That information allows them to make a salary offer they perceive to be adequate for you. Never mind that this offer more than likely won't take into consideration your immeasurable intellectual capital. **The company's objective is to pay the least amount for the highest value.** So whether you're able to run circles around your future co-workers and complete projects in a manner that reduces costs and increases value, none of that will matter. You will be paid based on the salary band of your employee peer group. And that usually will mean putting you in the middle of the band to allow room for incremental growth that comes with promotions.

Oftentimes, job candidates concentrate too much on the employment offer at the expense of the actual job duties. A great salary and benefits package are certainly nice to have but will mean little to your long-term success if you accept a job that does not leverage your value-adding ksa's. Too many job candidates are just happy to get an employment offer and assume that working out the details of the job can wait until the first day of work. This is part of the subtle deception of the salary and benefits you will be offered by the company. Your pay should be determined by the value of the job you perform and its impact on the bottom line of the department in which you will work. The majority of job candidates attempt to negotiate the total compensation but fail to negotiate expanding the duties of the job. It is the value of the job that will allow you to negotiate a higher compensation package. However, recruiters and Hiring Managers will not tell you this. They know that the salaries paid to most corporate employees do not fairly compensate them for the hours they work and the value they generate.

"You need to think in terms of compensation packages - including salaries, stock options, employee stock ownership plans, pay-for-performance plans, bonuses, profit sharing, commissions, noncash rewards, variable pay, and much more." - www.inc.com

The type of employment offer you are extended will depend upon many factors that you will not be privy to. However, one of the factors used will be whatever information you divulged regarding your salary history and salary expectations. This is the stage of the recruitment process where that information will come back to help you – or haunt you! The salary question trap is set early in the recruitment process in anticipation of using it against you later if you make it to the offer stage. This is a classic chess move that allows your opponent to be six moves ahead before you even realized the game began. If you were transparent with your salary details, then this is the stage where companies will use it against you. Even after receiving an employment offer, you will oftentimes not be told what the actual salary range is. The only time salary and total compensation should be discussed is after you have been extended a formal employment offer. Yet, recruiters will not tell you this and will have you believe that you must reveal the personal details of your salary history during the initial stages of the application process. This allows them to weaken your negotiating position while improving theirs.

How will you know if the initial employment offer is the company's best offer? You won't – and that's the company's objective. It's unfortunate that companies are not more transparent by just providing you with the salary ranges for their job postings before you apply. That would at least remove a lot of the secrecy and guesswork around how the job is valued and give you an opportunity to make the best decision. As it stands in regards to the employment offer, companies have an information advantage since they already know the budget for the job; however, you are left to play guessing games. Since your objective is to become an employee with the company, you don't want to lose a possibly good job opportunity. With publicly traded companies, all investors are supposed to have the same access to a company's financial information as they are made public. Company insiders are not supposed to share (or use for their own benefit) information that has not been made public to give a stockholder an unfair advantage. Unfortunately, these rules don't apply to the recruitment process as you usually will not know the compensation history of inside employees – excluding the C-suite – nor the other job candidates competing against you. Yet, recruiters and Hiring Managers are able to benefit from information which you are not privy to.

"Offers are extended live via telephone or in-person from a member of our internal team. If you are not selected for a particular role after your

interview, you will receive communication from a member of our team."
– Pepsi Co

Some (very few) recruiters are transparent with the salary packages for their job postings. Others might disclose it if you ask at the appropriate time after having advanced in the recruitment process; others are likely to stall you on the details of the salary range for a job until you are extended an employment offer; and others will simply state that the salary ranges are confidential. Nonetheless, they will not hesitate to request your salary and compensation history before extending you an employment offer. Ultimately, it is the Hiring Manager – not the recruiter (or responsible Human Resources professional) – who will determine your salary, additional compensation, and job duties. Discussions on salary and compensation are always sensitive because neither you nor the company wants to be taken advantage of. Therefore, when you receive an employment offer, you will need to meditate on *"The Holy Trinity of Employment Offers"* before finalizing any decision.

1. **The OMG! Employment Offer.** This is the "Oh My God!" employment offer that is so good that you will joyfully accept it upon receipt. Job candidates rarely receive this type of offer so when they do, they can count themselves among the few and the proud. The company has done all the hard work for you by meeting (or exceeding) your salary and compensation expectations. Rest assured that the company will extract its pound of flesh from you in exchange for this great offer. But that should be okay because at least you are being well compensated to do a job that has been properly valued. The companies that make these types of offers clearly understand the value you bring to them and the value of the job itself to the organization. A word of advice: try not to sound too overjoyed with the offer or the company might think it has overpaid you.

2. **The WTF! Employment Offer.** This is the "What The Fu@k!" employment offer that is so bad that you will leave it

on the table without even looking back. It is so low and so inadequate that you know it isn't even worth your time to try a negotiation. These offers define low-balling at its worst and are only focused on getting the cheapest employee rather than the highest value employee. Companies making these offers usually get what they pay for in terms of high employee turnover and the costs associated with continuously recruiting to fill the same positions. This is a strategy for some companies and they are fine with paying the extra recruitment costs while keeping their workforce salaries low. You'll be better served by walking away from these employment offers as they'll usually do your career more harm than good. If the company is keen to invest so little in you in the beginning, then chances are slim that they'll invest more in you later.

3. **The BRB Employment Offer.** This is the "Be Right Back" employment offer that is adequate enough that you will seriously consider it and think about ways to negotiate a win-win. This type of offer is not too cold and not too hot, but neither is it just right. Still, with a little massaging, this employment offer can be improved to yours and the company's benefit. One caveat: under no circumstances should you attempt to negotiate with the recruiter! Candidates desiring a better offer will need to present a convincing proposal directly to the Hiring Manager (their future boss). The Hiring Manager is always in a much better position than you to convince the Human Resources Director to make a modification. There will have to be some give and take on both sides which may involve discussions of non-monetary compensation components such as: vacation days, job titles, early performance reviews, specialized training, and anything else you value. If done properly, the negotiation can lead to an improvement in the job function and its benefit to the employer that will result in a win-win. Just make sure that you are really able to deliver on what you say.

It will be up to you to place a value on yourself before being extended an employment offer. This value should be the sum total of all the information you have learned about the company's business, its workplace environment, and how the job itself supports the success of its departmental unit (as well as the overall business). The candidates without a clue of the monetary value of their knowledge, skills, and abilities – or how the local market values them – will be at the mercy of a company's standard employment offer. The employment offers received in the corporate recruitment process are standard packages that you will not be able to alter drastically. The purpose of the recruitment process is not only to find the standard corporate employee, but also to pay the standard compensation package. Without these standards in place, companies cannot properly control and predict workforce costs that would seriously jeopardize the earnings of the CEO's and major shareholders. Global companies have shown that they will restructure and right-size before their CEO's and shareholders take a financial hit. Therefore, you can expect to receive a compensation package designed to contain costs – not reward value.

Chapter 16
Don't Waste Time Applying To Jobs Online

"He who joyfully marches to music in rank and file has already earned my contempt. He has been given a large brain by mistake, since for him the spinal cord would surely suffice." – Albert Einstein

If you look at the entirety of the corporate recruitment process and its embedded web of trap doors, then you will appreciate the difficulty of getting extended an employment offer. It takes a Herculean effort to be the one job seeker to emerge victorious with an employment offer in tow. But how many job postings will you have to apply to in order to earn that single victory? Does it make sense for you to apply online to every job posting you're interested in? I highly doubt you'll get contacted for each application you submit, let alone advance through the successive stages of the formal recruitment processes. There is no shortage of "how to" books on navigating the corporate recruitment process. One search on Amazon.com or a walk down the career aisle of any large bookstore will verify that. In addition, there are thousands of blogs, podcasts, and YouTube videos all telling you how to successfully overcome every challenge you will face. And while you may be tempted to follow these strategies and tactics in pursuing your online job search, they are merely examples of what Russ Ackoff (author of "On Purposeful Systems") called, *"doing the wrong thing righter"*. Ackoff was not only a management thinker, but also an excellent communicator of his thoughts in pithy sentences:

- All of our problems arise out of doing the wrong thing righter.
- The more efficient you are at doing the wrong thing, the wronger you become.
- It is much better to do the right thing wronger than the wrong thing righter.
- If you do the right thing wrong and correct it, you get better.

The corporate recruitment process is rigged from the beginning. As soon as you apply online, you instantly start playing a game where the odds of winning are stacked against you. Most companies should go into the gaming business and make titles for PlayStation, Nintendo, and Xbox since they seem to have so much fun designing challenging, multi-level recruitment games. **But is your objective to do a job, or to play a game? Is your objective to get an interview, or to get hired?** The formal recruitment process is like driving a car on a one-way street: any obstacle can block the road and delay – or end – the trip. There is no going backwards to find another street to reach your destination. The majority of job seekers who follow the rules of the corporate recruitment process end up getting rejected. This is proven through various studies estimating that over 80% of jobs in the United States are filled through the hidden job market. And though the percentages will vary by country, I'm confident that they are still quite high.

"According to statistics, 80 percent of all jobs are never advertised; they are filled through networking, inside contacts, and word-of-mouth." – www.experience.com

"The "hidden job market" contains 80% of all job openings available but these great jobs go unadvertised. To find these jobs you must explore the "hidden job market." It's a proactive approach where you track down potential openings and actively follow up on leads. You won't find much competition for these "unadvertised jobs" so the extra effort to track them down is well worth it." – www.collegerecruiter.com

Despite those statistics, many job seekers continue to march in unison towards the same online job postings over and over while expecting different results – in effect, doing the wrong thing righter. The fact that a few job seekers experience success when applying online is no reason for the continued reliance on this method. This is actually a passive methodology that many job seekers like to confuse with an active, highly-productive job search. The fact that they are applying online to multiple jobs each week cannot be considered active – let alone productive! What they are doing, in fact, is adopting what job search consultants define as the "apply and wait" and "post and pray" strategies. All of this just equates to "fake hustle": meaning they are doing a lot of low percentage activity instead of doing what will actually get them hired. It makes no sense to follow that course of action in your job search. When you apply online, you relinquish all of your free will and become a mere puppet whose strings will be pulled by corporate recruiters throughout the recruitment process. They will make you walk through fire and sleep on a bed of spikes in order to prove whether you merit advancement in the recruitment process.

Recruiters really have no value for the time you invest in preparing your written application materials, researching their companies, and taking their standardized assessments. Your passion, commitment, and other intangibles can't be easily quantified when you initially apply online. The ATS can only attempt to calculate your fit based on conceptual text algorithms that process your application materials. Any dummy can pack his application with the right words and phrases to fool a software program. Therefore, it is quite easy for the best candidates to get overlooked since incompetent recruiters will happily take what the ATS gives them without attempting to do any deeper inspection. Since you are just one among many applicants for the same jobs, it is difficult for you to stand out and attract the attention of a recruiter who doesn't even know your name. Most job seekers who apply online will either be left with an automated rejection email or no response at all – meaning game over. If you really want to gauge your probability of success in the formal recruitment process, you should try asking 10 corporate employees how they found their current jobs. Chances are high that the majority will disclose that they used the hidden job market or had an inside track on a job posting.

"A range of procedures, including numerical and logical reasoning tests, interviews, team exercises and presentations, enables us to evaluate your individual skills and qualities and assess your potential against the requirements of the role. Several individuals will score you against the seven core competencies to ensure objectivity throughout the entire application and selection process." – UBS

"In 2010, SAS received more than 56,000 résumés and filled more than 700 positions." – SAS Corporation

In reality, it is not easy for the average job seeker to make it through the recruitment process and receive an employment offer. You will have an easier time getting accepted into Oxford University than getting hired through the formal channels of most global corporations where recruiters reign supreme and have unbridled power to determine who gets selected and who gets rejected. **Job seekers must never forget that recruiters are mainly concerned with following departmental policies and procedures – not proactively shopping their credentials to Hiring Managers.** If you don't want to play the shell game of online job postings, I suggest you stop the mindless customization of your résumé and cover letter (assuming you were even doing that!) and the filling out of "standard template" application fields. Free your mind from its ATS-induced stupor and invest more time in using the internet for "people searches" instead of "job searches". Follow the logic: people hire people, software does not. If you decide to go one-on-one with the corporate recruitment process, then prepare for battle against the imperial corporate recruiters at your own risk. However, it won't be a fair fight since they will use artificial intelligence (the ATS), EBHP, and countless standardized tests to control the battlefield. In order to make it to the end of the formal recruitment process and get extended an employment offer, you will have to execute a near flawless game plan – and be a near flawless candidate.

Level Three

Hiring Managers Do The Hiring

Chapter 17
The Targeted Job Search

"Obstacles don't have to stop you. If you run into a wall, don't turn around and give up. Figure out how to climb it, go through it, or work around it." – Michael Jordan

It should no longer be counterintuitive to avoid any and all contact with corporate recruiters. However, there are only two rare exceptions when it is acceptable to contact them. **Exception #1** is the case when the recruiter has a solid relationship with the Hiring Manager and is able (and willing) to introduce you. **Exception #2** is the case when the recruiter is the Hiring Manager. Getting hired has nothing to do with how many jobs you apply to; it has everything to do with how many Hiring Managers you pitch to. It is imperative for you to understand that companies don't hire people out of charity. In other words, a hiring decision won't be made because an employer wants to make a charitable contribution to society. With few exceptions, you will only be hired if you have convinced a Hiring Manager that you will produce more than you cost. In order to reach the Hiring Manager at your target companies, you'll need to develop an entirely new playbook that will be designed to bypass the corporate recruitment game altogether. And you'll need to answer the one question that virtually every business-minded Hiring Manager wants to know: *Why should I hire you?*

Very few job seekers skirt the rules of the formal recruitment process because they have been brainwashed into believing that it would be detrimental to their candidacy to disobey corporate recruiters. How do you win if you apply according to the recruiter's instructions only to find that nobody even reads your application? How do you win if a recruiter does not like your application and therefore does not forward it to a Hiring Manager? A recruiter would be lying if he states that 100% of his company's employees were hired through the formal recruitment process. Therefore, you have to constantly remind yourself that your objective is to get hired, not to enter into a recruitment process that is designed to find needles in a haystack. The formal recruitment process is full of flaws and glitches that will impede your job search campaign. You are expected to apply to companies whose employer value proposition you cannot accurately measure. You'll be left with a bad tummy ache after enduring rejection after rejection from unscrupulous recruiters obliging you to play a rigged game. While you rot in misery and despair, corporate recruiters will not even provide any formal alternative methods to be hired. It's either their way or the highway. Should you let your job search campaign be dictated by EBHP and online applications, or should you seek a method to cure your job search blues?

The targeted job search method is the cure to the corporate recruitment game blues. Don't think of the targeted job search as breaking the rules or not following the instructions laid out by recruiters. View it as an alternative search method that will allow you to present your value to the company. It is a method that is squarely focused on reaching the Hiring Managers at your target companies, and is much more strategic than merely applying online. Its motto is **"Networking for the Best, Online Applications for the Rest."** The targeted job search requires taking a business approach to your job search campaign. Instead of applying and waiting, you will be networking and creating. Job seekers who use the targeted search spend most of their time networking with the right people, interviewing the right people (and being interviewed by the right people), and pitching their projects/proposals (and themselves) to the right people. This approach allows them to eliminate the competition inherent in the traditional job search and improves their chances of being extended an employment offer. In order to avoid the failure experienced by most job seekers entering the corporate recruitment game, you will need to strategically avoid key aspects of it. Therefore, before you embark upon using the targeted job search method, there are a few rules you will need to follow.

1. **Avoid The Applicant Tracking System.** There are only two exceptions when it is acceptable to apply online. Exception #1

is when you have already interviewed with the Hiring Manager and have been told that the job is yours. In this case, completing the details of the online application is just cursory and the recruiter will process it per the Hiring Manager's request. Even if there are other job candidates to be interviewed, the recruiter will screen them out in order to comply with the Hiring Manager's wishes. Exception #2 is when you meet at least 75% of the job posting's requirements (experience, education, competence, and attitude) and feel confident that you can submit an application that will pass the recruiter's screens. In this case, it is highly unlikely that you'll find many job postings meeting that criterion: ensuring that you only apply online when the probability of being selected for an interview is high.

2. **Avoid Employee Referral Programs.** These seemingly innocuous programs are actually one-way tickets to the recruiter. Employee referral programs are almost always managed and overseen by Human Resources departments. While it significantly increases the probability that you will receive an interview, it won't be an exclusive interview. After all, you won't be the only one who gets a referral; and you most certainly won't prevent a recruiter from interviewing the pool of other suitable candidates mined from the ATS. You will still be made to go through the same steps in the recruitment process as those not receiving referrals. There is incentive for employees to refer you to the formal recruitment channels because of the cash reward (or other compensation) that accompanies a successful hire. However, you would be better served by asking these employees to refer you directly to the Hiring Manager first. If the Big Boss is impressed with you, then there is a high probability that you'll get the job (whether it's a posted one or not).

3. **Avoid Career Fairs.** This may seem counterintuitive to your job search goals; however, career fairs are nesting grounds for recruiters. The probability of meeting a Hiring Manager from your target companies is extremely low at these events. Even if

you could, you would never get the time (or the opportunity) to do more than the standard two-minute pitch used by other carbon copy job seekers. The recruiters at these fairs usually just direct you to apply online like the rest of the job seeker herd that were not preselected to be interviewed at the fair. The value-add you want to sell can't be effectively communicated in an environment with half-crazed job seekers running around with résumé-packed briefcases...all impatiently waiting to swarm the anti-decision making recruiters. There is only one exception to this rule: view career fairs as networking and professional development opportunities and you will find them more beneficial.

In the following chapters, you'll read about methods used in the targeted job search that will allow you to travel an alternative, self-created path to reach the Hiring Manager. The traditional job search focuses on positioning yourself as a job beggar to pass through a recruitment process designed by policy-minded corporate recruiters. In contrast, the targeted job search focuses on positioning yourself as a resource person to get extended employment offers by business-minded Hiring Managers. Indeed, the main focus of the targeted job search is to clearly define and brand your employee value proposition before undertaking any job search activity. This is an important step for positioning yourself to present the best case of your employee value proposition that answers the question: *Why should I hire you?* Instead of investing time studying how to answer standard interview questions and how to write the best job applications, you will study the business challenges for the target companies in which you desire to work. Instead of spending a day holed up in an Assessment Center being evaluated by teams of assessors, you will spend a day presenting business solutions to teams of decision makers. However, you must proceed with caution: **operating outside the rules of the corporate recruitment game will attract the attention of the Corporate Agents who have sworn to protect the system at all costs.**

Your ability to remain hidden from the Corporate Agents, and to outrun them, will determine whether or not you make it to the Hiring Manager. Corporate Agents are the antibodies produced by the corporate recruitment game's immune system to fight against the infiltration of savvy job seekers who dare to circumvent the orifice of the formal recruitment process in order to speak directly to a Hiring Manager. If you are caught by one, they will alert a corporate recruiter to your undercover operation. The number of Corporate Agents cannot be measured, and their resolve to maintain the integrity of the corporate recruitment game cannot be underestimated. They are as faceless as the recruiters to whom they informally report. They are the brainwashed corporate employees and Hiring Managers (the non-business minded sort) who will report you to the proper authorities – the incompetent corporate recruiters – without a second thought if you inquire about job opportunities (both listed and unlisted). They are the ignorant – but sometimes well-intentioned – networking contacts (both inside and outside your target companies) who have been brainwashed into believing that recruiters are the sole gatekeepers of talent acquisition. They cannot be reasoned with nor negotiated with; therefore, they must be avoided. They are identified only by their allegiance to the corporate recruitment game and strong belief that all potential employees be vetted by it – even if they themselves were not hired through it.

Chapter 18
Me Inc. Versus Me Too!

"Big companies understand the importance of brands. Today, in the Age of the Individual, you have to be your own brand." – Tom Peters

Before speaking to a Hiring Manager (or any influential networking contact), it is essential that you **view yourself as an independent business and behave in the same manner as a successful business – regardless of size.** This means you will need to consider yourself as "Me Incorporated" (Me Inc.) which will distinguish you from the carbon copy "Me Too" job seekers in the market place. Establishing Me Inc. is the equivalent of creating a solid career brand that defines the attributes that will add a measurable benefit to specific business challenges. Me Inc. is your career brand, and your career brand is Me Inc. Every job seeker has a career brand whether it is defined or not. The difference is in those who are conscious of their career brand value versus those who are not. Your career brand should define metrics for the following: 1) skills; 2) values; 3) interests; 4) professional competencies; and 5) personal attributes. When this information is used to build the foundation of Me Inc. it allows you to conduct a customized job search that leverages your unique value proposition. In today's market, the effort it takes to get hired by a company oftentimes requires the same traits that entrepreneurs use to start a company.

"Regardless of age, regardless of position, regardless of the business we happen to be in, all of us need to understand the importance of branding. We are CEOs of our own companies: Me Inc. To be in business today, our most important job is to be head marketer for the brand called You."
– Tom Peters

Many books in the marketplace purport to tell you how to establish your career brand and how to behave like a business – as if anyone can do it! If it were as easy as reading a book, the world would be filled with more entrepreneurs than employees. Entrepreneurs are a small minority because they are the providers, the owners, and the risk takers. They are also the ones who possess a clearly defined value proposition to offer to clients and stakeholders. They have unique brands that have a measurable value just as the product brands that are created and sold by companies. Becoming Me Inc. means that you can offer yourself as a product (or service) that clearly specifies the features and benefits you can offer to your target employers. However, in order to be effective you will need to quantify and qualify the value of Me Inc. For example, one approach to measuring the value of a business bases it upon income, assets, or competitive market size. Similarly, measuring the value of Me Inc. can be based upon your professional accomplishments, social network, and differentiating characteristics versus other job seekers in the market. It takes days, weeks, and sometimes months to identify all the unique qualities you possess that would be of value to prospective employers.

The targeted job search has to be conducted like an entrepreneurial startup in order for it to yield the maximum benefits. You won't have the structure of a defined, lock-step recruitment process to guide your every step; therefore, your campaign to reach a Hiring Manager will be defined by your own creativity and innovation. There is no one-size fits all approach to how an entrepreneur creates a startup, attracts investors, and grows its customer base. Similarly, entrepreneurial job seekers are tasked with creating Me Inc., attracting target employers, and growing their network. It will be up to you to identify which companies have the specific challenges for which Me Inc. is uniquely positioned to provide solutions. As Me Inc., you clearly distinguish yourself from the job seekers who only use the traditional job search. While their objective is to define their employment value in relation to a job posting, yours will be to define your employment value in relation to the value of Me Inc. Your ability to define the value of Me Inc. will determine the effectiveness of your targeted job search. None of your target companies will want to waste their time on a job seeker who has neither business objectives nor business solutions.

Job seekers who don't position themselves as Me Inc. are labeled by default as Me Too (low value knock-off products). Me Too-job seekers are routinely processed, time-stamped, and discarded from applicant tracking systems. Only a select few are ferried through the formal recruitment process if they meet the standard corporate employee profile. Whereas Hiring Managers predefine the benefit to be derived from a standard corporate employee, using the Me Inc. approach allows you to predefine the benefit you will deliver to the Hiring Manager. You will position yourself as an independent consultant who analyzes a company's business and offers unique solutions. In order to properly assess your value in the marketplace and your value to prospective employers, you will need to know how all of your personal and professional characteristics translate into a measurable benefit for which a company would be willing to pay. Just as every global corporation has a monetary value attached to it, so too does Me Inc. The value that Hiring Managers determine you are worth will be a reflection of the value you have convinced them that Me Inc. is worth: an amount that will be significantly influenced by how distinct it is from others in the same marketplace.

"Truly Superior, Differentiated Products" had an average 98% success rate and 53.5% market share, while "Me-Too" Products averaged an 18.4% success rate and 11.6% market share." – Robert G. Cooper

Many job seekers never define their career brand; they allow others to define it for them – usually to their detriment. You can't sell what you don't know you have, and you can't improve what you don't know needs improving. Would you rather have companies poke and prod you with their psychometric tests and assessments to define your career brand based on some arbitrary benchmark? Or would you rather take control of your own career brand and define it for yourself? There are several benefits to becoming Me Inc. and leveling the playing field when speaking with Hiring Managers. Your objective is to define those benefits and tailor each one to the needs of your target employers.

1. **Product Value And Deliverables.** Just as a company's products serve specific purposes and facilitate specific tasks, so too does your career brand meet a specific hiring need to tackle specific business challenges. Your product value is your career brand, and that allows you to clearly communicate the deliverables you are able to provide. Instead of chasing job postings that have no alignment with your core competencies, you will only focus on the ones that you are uniquely able to address. You will also be able to create new job opportunities that address the current needs of the Hiring Managers with whom you speak.

2. **Business To Business Communications.** Job seekers who are extremely knowledgeable in their field of expertise are able to have direct business conversations with Hiring Managers. You don't see consulting firms doing business development with corporate recruiters, do you? When you have something of value to offer a company that has challenges you are uniquely able to solve, you need to communicate directly with the business-minded Hiring Manager responsible for solving those challenges. Being able to articulate how you can positively impact business metrics that are important to the Hiring Manager will increase your chances of getting hired.

3. **Adaptability To Market Changes.** Businesses are constantly evolving as they try to adapt to ever-changing market conditions. Why then should a job seeker not adapt to new ways to get extended an employment offer? As Me Inc. you must also be able to adapt and stay abreast of competitive forces that affect your career brand and earning potential. Instead of applying to job postings, you need to analyze them to gather market intelligence in your field of expertise and to spot trends in employer-demanded skills. Job seekers who can do this are able to become thought leaders and present unforeseen opportunities to their target companies.

4. **Continuous Brand Improvement.** Total Quality Management is at the core of keeping Me Inc. distinguished from its

competitors in the job search marketplace. Job seekers who consistently evaluate themselves by using assessment tools are like companies that evaluate themselves through employee engagement surveys, ideal employer rankings, and customer satisfaction surveys. Top companies receive awards and recognition from third party organizations that validate their brands. If it's important to your target companies to distinguish themselves from their competition, then shouldn't you distinguish yourself from yours? While your competition has to sit in the waiting room of the online application office to await certification by a recruiter, your awards and recognition will ensure that you get escorted directly to a Hiring Manager's office!

There is no limit to the value you can present to a target employer when you identify yourself as Me Inc. When you embrace the fact that you are a company and begin to behave like a successful one, you will position yourself as someone who can speak confidently and directly to Hiring Managers. This will put you light-years ahead of the job seekers who focus mainly on preparing themselves to converse with gatekeeping recruiters. As Me Inc., you are presenting yourself as a resource person: someone who can combine innovation and creativity to positively impact business results. Try presenting Me Inc. in a formal recruitment process and you won't make it past the first incompetent recruiter who is tasked with inspecting your career brand – assuming the recruiter even knows what a career brand is! For this reason, presenting Me Inc. must only be done in the presence of learned individuals: the business-minded Hiring Managers. It is like the sharing of a fine cognac: it cannot be wasted on frivolous affairs.

Chapter 19
Professional Service Provider Versus Average Corporate Employee

"The greatest virtues are those which are most useful to other persons." – Aristotle

When you consider yourself a company, you will pursue the necessary activities that increase the value of your business. When you have a career brand, you are able to position yourself as a "Professional Service Provider" rather than an "Average Corporate Employee". The difference between the two is as different as night and day – only it will be up to you to communicate this to your target companies. **The average corporate employee is merely focused on the tasks and duties they are assigned:** with few exceptions, they will usually do no more and no less. They are not focused on the overall health of the business nor do they understand (or pay attention to) the metrics that drive business results. They have no concept of going above and beyond the call of duty, nor do they worry about the impact of their work on clients and customers. To them, work is just a place you go to get paid for a job someone else tells you to do. These types of employees would rather be someplace else – anywhere but on the job.

The average corporate employee lacks a career brand and the concept itself is foreign to them. They are more concerned with merely holding on to their jobs than benefiting the company in a measurable way. They are only focused on maintaining the status quo of their job duties and will not innovate or create beyond those duties. They live by their job descriptions and will make reference to them anytime they are asked to do a new task or duty. They cost their employers more by what they don't do than by what they actually do. In fact, if asked a simple question, *"What do you do for your company?"*, they are unable to tell you beyond rattling off a list of tasks and duties. They are, in effect, corporate drones that are incapable of doing anything of their own volition for fear of making a mistake. They are content to let someone else be responsible for the company's success and are loath to continuously improve themselves through informal training (although they will happily waste the company's money on formal training). Whether they are byproducts of a company's bureaucracy, or are just inherently incompetent, they will not look for ways to make the company money (or save money) unless they are explicitly told to do so.

Managers lose a lot of sleep over the average corporate employees. They become the doers in the corporate landscape – only they don't always "do" their jobs well. They are resigned to being the corporate drones who are tasked with completing the routine activities that keep the corporate ship afloat; however, they will be the first ones terminated as soon as the top brass find a way to automate their duties or outsource their jobs altogether. They have no professional direction and their jobs are merely substitutes for what they have yet to figure out is their professional calling. Since they don't know what job will get them on the road to professional fulfillment, any job will do – at a great cost to companies! It is for this reason that companies take measured steps to screen job seekers in the corporate recruitment process for any signs of becoming an "average corporate employee". However, it is odd that companies expend so much energy trying to avoid hiring the average corporate employee, when it is their own smothering blankets of bureaucracy that end up transforming talented new hires into the average corporate employee anyway.

"In business you get what you want by giving other people what they want." – Alice MacDougall

On the other end of the spectrum, **professional service providers are focused on affecting business results and improving stakeholder satisfaction.** They will keep up with the latest trends in their field of expertise and will prevent their employers from experiencing catastrophic failure. They are always focused on the health of the business and are constantly measuring the impact of their work. They understand how their unique skills impact the profitability of their departments and business units. Professional service providers have an entrepreneurial mindset: they are self-starters who can create new practices and modify existing ones to benefit the business. They are the Me Inc. workers who value improving the business metrics of their employers as much as they do their own career brands. They are concerned with the satisfaction of internal and external stakeholders, and work to improve upon metrics that measure their satisfaction through feedback and surveys. They are self-aware and clear on their professional calling which allows them to direct their skills in the areas that will best impact the company. They know the exact levers of an organization that they can positively affect to increase specific business metrics.

Professional service providers don't view their work as just a job, but rather, as a career. Therefore, they tie their success to the success of the company in which they work. They will put in the necessary time after standard work hours to complete a project before its deadline. They are the thinkers who protect their companies from unnecessary risks by asking the tough questions, and they are also the doers who deliver high quality project results. If I ask a simple question, *"What do you do for your company?"*, they will discuss the clear benefits they provide their employers through reducing product costs, increasing customer loyalty, delivering quality customer service, identifying competitive threats, improving the flow of team communications, and a host of other benefits that have a measured impact on the bottom line. They value their career brands and strive to provide top-notch service to all their stakeholders. They make suggestions on what a company can do better and take initiative before being told what to do. Professional service providers are not merely focused on the tasks and duties assigned by their Hiring Manager. They evolve their responsibilities by going above and beyond what is asked of them. Managers can sleep well at night when they hire workers with the mentality of professional service providers.

The majority of job seekers will become average corporate employees due to myriad factors both within and outside their control. The few job seekers who will become the professional service providers of their target employers will be tasked with differentiating themselves during their targeted job search. If you want to impress Hiring Managers and members of your network, presenting yourself as a professional service provider will display your ability to:

1. **Identify Current Business Challenges.** The job seekers who have identified their career brands know how to apply those same self-analysis skills to identify their target companies' current challenges. Being able to identify a company's challenges allows professional service providers to offer custom solutions. Just as consulting firms have areas of expertise and develop reputations for being able to solve specific challenges, likewise do professional service providers. Speaking with a Hiring Manager will be a lot more productive when you can speak confidently about your ability to provide specific solutions to challenges you know they are facing.

2. **Identify Future Business Challenges.** The ability to aggregate data from diverse sources, analyze it, and predict how it will affect a business is not an ability possessed by the average job seeker. There are dedicated professional service firms that only focus on analyzing data and predicting future trends. Some large companies have departments dedicated to this in the form of risk analysis and new product development. The job seekers who have the unique ability to see future challenges can give their target companies a competitive advantage. Being able to speak with Hiring Managers about challenges yet to affect their companies will create a lot of interest and likely lead to an employment offer.

Your ability to position yourself as a professional service provider will offer many distinct advantages over the job seekers positioned as average corporate employees. It will provide a huge boost to your employment prospects and allow you to anticipate the needs of your target companies. The corporate recruitment process is little more than a crapshoot for many talented job seekers who have a professional service provider mindset. It is too easy for them to get lost in the ATS database if they don't have the standard profile. Sorting them accordingly is left to the competency of the recruiter managing the recruitment process. This is not a risk you should be willing to take given the ubiquity of incompetent recruiters. Instead of wasting time becoming expert at completing online applications and going through lock-step recruitment processes, your time will be better spent when you brainstorm ideas on how to add value to your target employers. When your job search becomes an entrepreneurial venture that is independent of any formal recruitment process, you will seek out opportunities to provide services to the target companies that will most benefit from what you are uniquely able to deliver.

Chapter 20
Net-working Versus Not-working

"It isn't just what you know, and it isn't just who you know. It's actually who you know, who knows you, and what you do for a living." – Bob Burg

Networking is the lifeblood that is essential to conducting a successful targeted job search campaign. If you are not networking to find a job or networking to advance in your current career, then you are **NOT-working!** Unless you are so good and so well-known that the world beats a path to your doorstep, you will need to have a healthy online (and face-to-face) positioning and networking strategy. No matter the stage of your career, you must establish an online identity that promotes your career brand so that you are visible to employers and to those from whom you are seeking advice and referrals. **Networking is to a job seeker what business development is to a company.** Business development involves at minimum the ability to identify gaps in the marketplace, attract new customers, and penetrate existing markets. These are the same abilities needed to effectively network in order to position your career brand to meet the needs of your target companies.

"Because the vast majority of job openings are never advertised, job-seekers need to have a network of contacts -- a career network -- that can provide support, information, and job leads." – www.quintcareers.com

Many job seekers falsely view networking as an activity used only to communicate their job search goals. They have their résumés and two-minute pitches so prepared and rehearsed that they sound more like pre-programmed drones than value-adding service providers. Bombarding people in that manner is a recipe for disaster. Job seekers who engage in that practice are the ones who typically spend more hours each day applying online – which by the way, is not-working – than meeting new people or rekindling relationships with existing associates. Getting an audience with a Hiring Manager will be dependent upon your ability to strategically position your career brand and network in order to reach the right people with the right message. Networking for a job is about building trust and reliability around mutual interests to the benefit of all stakeholders in your physical and virtual community. Your networking must be strategic in order to connect with the right people in the right positions, and not waste time with the wrong people in the right positions.

Who are the right people to connect with? The answer is the Hiring Managers and Influence Peddlers. The need to connect with Hiring Managers is already apparent, though it is oftentimes easier said than done. Therefore, you have to connect with people who are accessible and wield substantial influence on the Hiring Managers at your target companies: these people are called the Influence Peddlers. They are the people in your network who are able to get you past the gatekeeping recruiters. They are also the people whom Hiring Managers hold in high regard, and can be either internal or external to your target companies. Think of Influence Peddlers as the equivalent of the lobbyists and special interest groups you find at any political establishment: they have the ability and means to sway the opinion of the real decision makers. Most job seekers are so brainwashed nowadays that they don't even feel worthy enough to speak directly to a Hiring Manager, let alone an Influence Peddler. Don't fall into this trap! You don't have to kiss the ring finger of a recruiter in order to gain access to the corporate spoils. While getting an audience with the Hiring Managers is job #1, don't overlook the power of the Influence Peddlers who can get you a front row seat.

"The greatest ability in business is to get along with others and to influence their actions." – John Hancock

Influence Peddlers will gladly promote your brand if you indeed have something of value to offer. The payback to the Influence Peddlers is in adding value to their own network and solidifying their standing as a resource. Hiring Managers are human and can therefore be influenced by the people they trust and respect. In rare cases, an Influence Peddler can be a recruiter or anyone in the Human Resources department. But more than likely they will reside outside the hallowed halls of the HR department – thank goodness! You need to spend just as much time trying to connect with Influence Peddlers as you do with Hiring Managers; however, keep in mind that not all Hiring Managers and Influence Peddlers are business-minded talent identifiers. Many of them are Corporate Agents who will stonewall you until the recruiter comes to investigate your "attempted break-in" of the Hiring Manager's chambers. Therefore, use social media and informational interviewing to do a thorough background check on the networking contacts who are most likely to value your career brand. These will be the ones who will gladly assist your journey to meet directly with a Hiring Manager instead of throwing you to the wolves of the formal recruitment process.

"Professional networking is about making contacts and building relationships that can lead to jobs or other work-related opportunities. Thoughtful networking provides a focused way to talk to people about your job search." – www.career-advice.monster.com

Networking provides the multiple routes needed to bypass the formal recruitment process and make it to the Hiring Manager. It is indeed the heart of a targeted job search campaign that pumps constant communications to the key people who can contribute to your professional success. How long would Mckinsey & Company stay in business if it ceased doing business development? Even with their brand position, could they really afford to stop talking to potential clients and engaging existing ones? Certainly not! If they can't do it, neither can you. **Strategic networking with the right people and positioning yourself with the right activities are the keys to promoting your career brand and engaging with your target companies.** Many job seekers using the traditional job search method simply believe that networking is just the mindless task of randomly contacting people at their target companies to inquire about job opportunities – or worse, blindly send them résumés. The targeted job search utilizes networking as a business tool that allows you to position yourself as a person of interest who can benefit your target companies. Make the most of networking in your job search campaign by:

1. **Becoming Recognized As A Field Expert.** Too many job seekers believe they can only become experts in something by working for someone else. If this were true, then there would be no Mark Zuckerberg, Bill Gates, Steve Jobs, or Michael Dell among many, many others. You can become an expert by having a relentless commitment to something you want to do and know more about. You will be taken seriously by companies when you behave like successful companies. It's important to position yourself as a recognized expert by collaborating with other recognized experts in your field. By having something of value to contribute to the body of knowledge in a specific field, you are able to bolster your status as an expert in that area.

2. **Selecting The Channels For Career Brand Promotion.** Find the right opportunities to participate in that will showcase your career brand to your target audience. Social media tools offer a low-cost and extremely effective way to accomplish this objective. You could promote yourself through online networks, blogs, podcasts, videocasts, webcasts, whitepapers, books, and any other channels that best align with your career brand. Promoting through multiple channels doesn't mean that you are just relegated to the information you upload and share online. It also includes the content you deliver offline in the form of speeches delivered at community events, professional organizations, and volunteering activities connected to your career goals (and valued by your target companies). Oftentimes the offline strategic networking in your community can lead to collaborations with advisory boards, recognition awards, and special projects. It is usually through these relationships that you will meet either a Hiring Manager or Influence Peddler.

3. **Communicating Value-Adding Information.** Many job seekers are just "downloaders" of online and offline

information. They don't add to the treasure chest as much as they take from it for their own personal gain. To establish your value, you should give as much as you get, and act as an "uploader" of your intellectual property for the benefit of others. Strategic networking means that you don't merely leech off the expertise of others, but rather, you complement it: this will be done through your contributions to online discussion boards and sharing of relevant information. For example, through blogging, you can encounter other bloggers who are experts in the same field with whom you can share information. Through these relationships come the opportunities to write for popular blogs or online magazines that will increase your career brand recognition. This approach is replicated for the other online and offline forums where you seek to establish yourself as a reliable source of information.

4. **Establishing Relationships With Target Companies.** Companies that offer crowdsourcing projects and problem-solving challenges for various issues facing their businesses offer excellent opportunities for job seekers to connect. Participation in these activities provides an excellent way to build your expertise and to get recognized by the company for your contribution. Another way to establish a relationship with targeted companies is to do original and independent research related to a current challenge they face. You could then write a whitepaper (or article) to publish to popular online sites where others share their know-how and expertise. This opens the opportunity to discuss the feedback you'll receive on your writings as well as a conversation starter with company (and industry) insiders. It is important to find ways to benefit your target companies on the issues and challenges that are important to them. The more engaged you are with the challenges that affect your target companies, the more likely it is that you will form relationships with people who can aid your job search. These are the relationships that will get you on a first name basis with Hiring Managers and Influence Peddlers.

There are many networking strategies that will position you as the candidate of choice for your targeted companies. You will need to choose the methods that best fit your personality and comfort zone. Patience and perseverance must be the hallmarks of your networking strategy, otherwise you will not gain the trust of the people whose assistance you will need. You will be successful when you focus on increasing the equity, visibility, and relevance of your career brand among your target audiences. Networking is as much an art as it is a science, and can be done effectively both online and offline. Choose wisely where you position yourself and how you promote information that validates and solidifies your career brand. Every activity you engage in must be beneficial not only to you, but also to the network you support. As you network with new contacts who can move you closer to meeting with a Hiring Manager, you will have to become adept at distinguishing friend from foe. In the movie, *The Matrix*, anyone who was not unplugged from the system was a potential agent whose sole job was to protect the system. The same holds true for corporations and the people who are stakeholders in their survival: anyone brainwashed by employer branding hocus pocus is a potential Corporate Agent. They will pose as potential allies in your networking campaign, only to re-route you to the first recruiter they can find – oftentimes an incompetent one!

Chapter 21
Marketing Portfolios Versus Traditional Résumés

"The aim of marketing is to know and understand the customer so well the product or service fits him and sells itself." – Peter F. Drucker

To modify a popular line from the Humphrey Bogart film, *The Treasure of the Sierra Madre*, "you don't need no stinking résumé!" While the job seekers who waste time applying online spend hours and hours customizing "Traditional Résumés" in order to get through the applicant tracking system and in front of the eyes of a recruiter, you'll get better results by creating a "Marketing Portfolio". I could probably write a book that lists all of the books that have been published on writing the perfect résumé! And most of them have the same purpose of directing you to apply online like an obedient job seeker to be processed like a block of cheese. **A traditional résumé, no matter how perfectly it may be written, obliges people to focus on your past at the expense of your future.** It encapsulates your body of work into a 1-2 page document that only serves to highlight your past glory. It bases discussions on what you did for a past (or current) company versus what you can do for your target companies. At every turn in your networking efforts to reach Hiring Managers at your target companies, you will be faced with Corporate Agents requesting your résumé. They will not even inquire about how you can be a value-add to their companies since they are programmed to believe that the traditional résumé will suffice.

"Most candidates put together a generic resume, all about them, with what they think is important and relevant, then cross their fingers and hope it gets to the reader's underlying motivations. It rarely if ever does." – www.boomersnextstep.com

While companies adapt web 2.0 technologies to sell their products and build brand loyalty, it is puzzling that corporate recruiters still oblige job seekers to primarily sell themselves with traditional résumés. While the traditional résumé itself is not dead, it is indeed passé. It is held up as the gold standard only by the corporate recruiters who still base their livelihoods on using it as the preferred method to determine which job seekers pass through the pearly gates of the ATS. There are entire industries that have sprung up around the development of résumés: software vendors who sell applicant tracking systems, authors who write how-to books, and consultants who provide résumé writing services. They are the only stakeholders who benefit more from the traditional résumé than job seekers do. It's a bit of a stretch to assume that the average job seeker can write a résumé that will appeal to the particular biases of an unknown recruiter or Hiring Manager. Most résumés are written with the intent to apply online or to attend career events. They are usually tailored to the needs identified in a job posting instead of the needs identified by a Hiring Manager – big difference! When you have your sights set squarely on speaking directly with a Hiring Manager instead of going through the multi-level stages of the formal recruitment process, you'll need to arm yourself with a different type of sales tool – the marketing portfolio.

Job seekers who spend too much time trying to craft the perfect résumé end up leaving their fates in the hands of a recruiter to sort out what is relevant and what is not. Even a Hiring Manager can get confused by a traditional résumé no matter how customized it is to fit his needs – there is only so much you can do with a static document. And adding web links to a static document does not make it dynamic or any more tailored to the Hiring Manager's specific concerns. In contrast, **the marketing portfolio is a dynamic communications tool that states clearly what you can do to meet the company's current and future needs.** Instead of following the cookie-cutter two-step process of résumés and cover letters – which can only describe what you've done and what you want to do respectively – the marketing portfolio uses web 2.0 technologies to connect you directly with your networking contacts and the Hiring Manager. It is an amalgamation of social media-driven evidence of your competence and expertise in a specific area of value to the company. It tells the story of what challenges you are qualified to solve and supports those statements with substantial proof. These portfolios focus less on your chronological work history, and more on your ability to meet the pressing needs faced by your target companies.

"You can have the best product or service in the world, but if people don't buy - it's worthless. So in reality it doesn't matter how wonderful your new product or service is. The real question is - will they buy it?" – Noel Peebles

When using a traditional résumé, you instantly make the discussion about your past as it pertains to other companies and entities. The discussion then becomes less about what you can do for the Hiring Manager and more about how you handled past situations. Why waste the precious time you have to convince someone to hire you by babbling about situations that don't address current and specific pain points? Don't expect a recruiter or Hiring Manager to look beyond the traditional résumé to determine your fit. Be proactive and present them with the marketing portfolio! Your marketing portfolio should include your social media footprints that qualify and quantify your subject matter expertise in the areas in which your career brand is built. This is a key premise to establishing a business-to-business dialogue with a Hiring Manager. It's not all about what you say regarding your expertise, but what others say regarding your expertise. Marketing portfolios are more effective when they include information that is:

1. **Relevant To Common Industry Challenges.** Every industry has its share of challenges and your job is to identify the ones in which you have recognized expertise or experience. For example, if the common challenge in the Oil and Gas Industry is to expand the use of clean energy and alternative fuels, then your portfolio will contain the appropriate print and digital proof attesting to your competence to meet those challenges.

2. **Relevant To Specific Company Challenges.** Some companies have unique challenges that are not widespread throughout the industry. For example, if Google is experiencing challenges from the French government regarding copyright

infringement of books authored by French writers, then your portfolio will contain any documents that support your expertise in digital media, copyright law, and e-commerce.

3. **Relevant To Strategic Business Unit Challenges.** As you research your target companies you will find challenges that are specific to certain business units within those companies. For example, if Samsung's Latin American Operations is having difficulty gaining a foothold for its tablet computers in Brazil, then your portfolio will contain any information that supports your knowledge of Brazilian culture, language, market demographics, etc.

4. **Relevant To Competitive Group Challenges.** In this case, think of the business challenges facing Apple, Amazon, Google, and Facebook that have each company looking over their shoulders. For example, if you have expertise in designing mobile apps or developing businesses that use cloud software, then you can provide that proof in your portfolio to bolster your case as a candidate of choice.

Your marketing portfolio should provide all the supporting proof of your ability to provide business solutions to pre-existing and future challenges. Through the use of social media, you can measure the value of your portfolio's contents and provide a more insightful view of your expertise. For example, if you have written extensively about clean energy reform or have given recorded presentations on the subject, you can use Twitter, Facebook, and LinkedIn (among others) to measure its reception. The marketing portfolio only addresses the specific needs of your target companies in the same way that a company uses marketing brochures and digital advertising campaigns to sell to target demographics. The advertising campaigns of the top companies are not littered with irrelevant information like most traditional résumés. Instead, they are designed to appeal to the specific needs of target customers. In contrast, using a traditional résumé forces you to list past work experiences that are not always relevant to your target companies. Given the fact that constant changes in technology and the global market present an ever-evolving array of business challenges to companies, it is no longer reliable to use past results to predict future success.

Nowadays, you have to think outside the box when trying to sell your career brand to a prospective employer. Endeavor to market yourself to companies in 15-30 second advertisements just like companies market to you on television, radio, YouTube, and other online media. It's more engaging and guaranteed to set you apart from your competitors in the job market. The objective of the marketing portfolio is to grab the attention of the Hiring Managers so that they want to learn more about you. Which do you think will have the biggest impact: Sending an article you wrote on a relevant business challenge that was published by a reputable magazine and tweeted 500 times?; or 2) Sending a traditional résumé and leaving it up to the Hiring Manager to find the line item you dedicated to that relevant business challenge buried among the other content? The former shows how the market validates your subject matter expertise along with the value that it assigns to it, while the latter only states the accomplishment as you describe it along with the value that you assign to it. You usually have one shot to impress a Hiring Manager – make it count!

It is time to put the traditional résumé in its proper place once and for all: the Smithsonian Institution. It's an antiquated document whose time has passed, and serves no useful purpose other than to keep job seekers tied to the puppet strings of the corporate recruitment game. Using a traditional résumé in the 21st century is equivalent to a company spending 80% of its advertising budget on print media – it's so 1990's! Unless your objective is to meet a recruiter for a fireside chat, there is little upside to creating a traditional résumé. It's up to you to change the tastes of your potential consumers (Hiring Managers) and get them hooked on a new way of assessing your talents. At one time, the music industry executives from Warner Music Group and EMI fought against the rising tide of consumer demand for downloadable music. While they continued to sell a format that was profitable to them but inconvenient to consumers, Apple Corporation stepped in with the iPod and created an entire industry from which the traditional music industry has yet to recover.

"Marketing whether in print or electronically doesn't try and attract everyone with one advertisement. Companies well known as "marketing" companies, Nike, Coke, McDonalds, and Apple have multiple ads each with a specific purpose to reach a specific customer. They are very targeted with the listener's or reader's motivations in mind. They rarely if ever assume one-size-fits-all." – www.boomersnextstep.com

Don't let a reliance on traditional résumés derail your ultimate objective: getting hired. You will find that most Hiring Managers will probably prefer a traditional résumé because that is what they have been accustomed to using as the measuring stick of talent assessment. Corporate recruiters continue to promote the traditional résumé to Hiring Managers as well as train them on how to assess it. Your mission will be to present a new way for Hiring Managers to judge you by showing the marketing portfolio as a superior alternative. Just as Google and Facebook have transformed the way advertising is done, you can also use the same concepts to transform the way hiring is done. Advertisers want the most bang for their buck, and do not want to spend money blasting countless messages in media outlets that are not frequented by their target audiences. Furthermore, they want to customize their message to meet their targets' specific needs. The same business strategy applies to the targeted job search. Social media technologies allow you to present attention-grabbing messages to the Hiring Managers at your target companies, and will provide them more real-time content attesting to your bid as an employee of choice.

Chapter 22
Personal Endorsements Versus Passive Referrals

"Referrals aren't given easily. If you don't take the time to establish credibility, you're not going to get the referral. People have to get to know you. They have to feel comfortable with who you are and what you do." – Ivan Misner

During the targeted job search, you'll endure many roadblocks and challenges as you continue your journey to reach the mythical Hiring Manager. Much like Dorothy's trip to meet the *Wizard of Oz*, the path will be littered with traps, distractions, and illusions. Corporate recruiters are the biggest purveyors of the hijinks that will delay your journey. They will use Corporate Agents to go out on search and destroy missions to derail you: your underground railroad to the Hiring Manager will be under constant attack. One ploy that has become the favorite among recruiters is the use of Corporate Agents to refer top job seekers. Every recruiter and Hiring Manager recognizes the power of the "referral" as it pertains to meeting the right job candidates. As such, companies have created their own referral system, dubbed the "employee referral program", to take advantage of this tried and true practice. The logic is that job seekers referred by Corporate Agents are more likely to be successful in the confines of the corporate construct. While there is much truth in that premise, the challenge for job seekers using the traditional job search is to get an employee referral from the right Corporate Agent at their target companies: otherwise, it's a useless program. **The challenge for job seekers using the targeted job search is to avoid the employee referral program altogether.**

The major flaw with employee referral programs is that they are one-way tickets to the bosom of a corporate recruiter. You'll find that for all its glory and radiance, the employee referral program just puts you on the front line of an open recruitment process where you'll have the (dis)honor to speak with a recruiter. Of course, your only intention should be to speak directly to a Hiring Manager – not a recruiter – so the employee referral program is really just another sticky patch meant to delay your journey on the yellow brick road. In rare cases, the program works: only when an employee actually advocates your candidacy directly to a Hiring Manager. Employee referrals can be categorized into two types: 1) Personal Endorsements; 2) Passive Referrals. These can come from current employees or influential non-employees, but you'll need to understand which type of referral is given on your behalf before you can move forward. It goes without saying that a referral given through an employee referral program cannot be compared to a personal endorsement. Why? Because there is nothing personal about an employee referral program! It is indeed nothing more than a "passive referral program" that only encourages Corporate Agents to register members of their personal network (those who best fit the standard corporate employee mold) in hopes of collecting some financial (or non-financial) reward.

"Referral programs are essentially marketing programs and as a result, they lose their effectiveness over time. In fact, even the best designed programs begin to produce significantly lower results in as little as six months if the marketing materials and approach are not updated." - www.ere.net

"It's not unusual for regular recruiters to ignore or pay little attention to candidates who come from employee referrals. It's generally an ego thing because they didn't initially "find" the candidate." - www.ere.net

"If all individuals being referred are required to visit the corporate website in order to apply, there is a significant chance that the source of the resume will not be "marked" as a referral. In fact, some HR technology does not allow referrals to be "marked" so that they can be given higher priority." - www.ere.net

Passive referrals are worthless! The above quotes are proof that even the most well-intentioned employee referral programs can go awry. Avoid these passive referrals (and the Corporate Agents who give them) at all costs! These are the people who just request your résumé in order to forward it to a recruiter whom they don't even know. In the best case, an employee will register your name using a formal process designated by the Human Resources department. In the worst case, your materials will be forwarded to a general email designated by the Human Resources department. The person making the referral isn't putting any personal testimonies behind it, or getting from behind a computer screen to lobby on your behalf. **Therefore, the only referral that is worth having is a personal endorsement from a Trusted Source.** These endorsements are from people (internal or external to the target company) who will go the extra mile on your behalf by speaking directly with the Hiring Manager to give him a personal testimony of your value. Additionally, the Trusted Source will make sure the Hiring Manager personally contacts you instead of handing it off to some random recruiter. Doesn't that sound much more beneficial to you than some employee referral program that will just ensure – at most – that you get an interview with an unknown recruiter?

"Those who make the actual hiring decisions would much rather talk to someone who has been recommended by someone they already employ. This is your first reference check, which saves the hiring manager considerable effort sorting through all the resumes and phone calls an advertisement will generate." – www.rileyguide.com

Trusted Sources won't sell you out to a recruiter because they understand how the corporate recruitment game operates. They are anathema to corporate recruiters and are your allies in the fight against the Corporate Agents trying to sabotage your mission. They are not brainwashed by employer branding hocus pocus and have witnessed the shortcomings of the formal recruitment process: recruiters are only concerned with hiring standard corporate employees versus *bona fide* solutions providers. Trusted Sources understand the value of talent, and will personally endorse you to the appropriate Hiring Manager instead of risking your candidacy in the employee referral program. They know that the only advantage of the employee referral program is to guarantee that a recruiter actually sees your résumé – after you apply online, of course. They are business-minded and will think of how your talents can benefit an organization whether they are employed there or not. They have built successful career brands and powerful networks for themselves which add extra weight to their personal endorsements. They are not easily impressed, and will not put their necks on the line for just any job seeker breaking the rules of the formal recruitment process. Indeed, an incompetent rules breaker not measuring up to their standards will be politely instructed to go apply online.

Developing a strong connection with a Trusted Source will take patience and perseverance: they don't just give personal endorsements away like raffle tickets. However, they do provide the ticket to bypass the minefield-laden corporate recruitment process. Personal endorsements are essential to many of the business transactions played out in the global marketplace every day. Think about it, you are more likely to purchase products recommended by your social network than from some unknown entity. If you need to have your car repaired, would you go to the mechanic endorsed by your friend, or choose the one with the fancy advertisements and testimonies from people you don't know? People rely on the experiences of others in order to make decisions on how they will best spend their money. For this reason, your ability to forge trust-based relationships with your network will dictate the strength of the personal endorsements you are able to obtain. The best ones will present you to Hiring Managers as a value-add for the company. If you are able to build a strategic network and skillfully position your career brand, then you will be able to use the following personal endorsement strategies to get a direct conversation with a Hiring Manager.

1. **Endorsements From Well-Regarded Company Associates.** Job seekers who build relationships with respected associates working at their target companies are in a good position to get endorsed. If you spend significant time on activities that add value to your network, then you will be comfortable requesting personal endorsements from those associates. Oftentimes, well-regarded company associates will reach out to you when you properly manage and promote your career

brand in line with what your target companies value. Smart and highly-productive people enjoy working with others of the same ilk who will be just as committed to tackling the myriad challenges faced in the global market.

2. **Endorsements From External Company Stakeholders.** These stakeholders can be vendors, contractors, non-profits, etc., that are connected to companies targeted by job seekers. Job seekers who have invested in activities positioning them to interact with these entities are able to get personal endorsements from company-approved sources. In many cases, these endorsements are just as strong as the ones from a well-regarded company associate. Oftentimes these stakeholders have long histories with their partner companies and are deeply involved in their success. The strength of the endorsement you receive will be directly proportional to the value you have added to the activities of the stakeholder.

3. **Endorsements From Networking Associates.** Sometimes, job seekers might have someone in their network that has a strong relationship with a company associate of interest. In this case, they are able to leverage the network effect and rely on the strength of their primary contact to build a bridge through secondary and higher contacts. Though oftentimes not as strong as the endorsement from a primary contact, they still yield results. These endorsements facilitate reaching Hiring Managers at target companies outside your primary network. Leading companies rely on word of mouth to endorse and sell their products. And you too should rely on word of mouth to endorse and sell your career brand.

"Some managers may have biases against employee-referral programs, feeling that referrals are favors done for shiftless in-laws rather than for the company." – www.hrworld.com

Anyone can get an employee referral (a.k.a. passive referral) to speak directly with a corporate recruiter, but anyone can't get a personal endorsement to speak directly with a Hiring Manager. The personal endorsement serves as the validation that companies try to ascertain when poking and prodding job seekers with the various assessments used in the formal recruitment process. Recruiters could care less about a personal endorsement and will dutifully follow HR protocol by putting job seekers through the same recruitment process as those without personal endorsements. Therefore, personal endorsements are more valuable in the targeted job search because they are only given on your behalf to Hiring Managers and Influence Peddlers. If you lack an influential network that values your career brand, then you will have difficulty getting personal endorsements beyond the passive "résumé forward" facilitated by Corporate Agents: they will only forward it to the attention of an unknown recruiter in the HR department. In contrast, the Trusted Sources will facilitate an active "résumé forward" to the Hiring Manager followed up by a phone call or face-to-face meeting. Trusted Sources just won't tell the story on your behalf, they will also sell the story and advocate your employment candidacy.

Chapter 23
Pitching For Projects Versus Interviewing For Jobs

"If I am to speak ten minutes, I need a week for preparation; if fifteen minutes, three days; if half an hour, two days; if an hour, I am ready now." – Woodrow Wilson

Every preceding step in the targeted job search campaign was designed to establish yourself as a business-oriented solutions provider; identify and position your brand with strategic networking contacts; develop a marketing portfolio that provides proof of your ability to address specific challenges at your target companies; and obtain the right personal endorsements that will facilitate an invite to speak with a Hiring Manager. Once you get the green light to meet directly with a Hiring Manager, it is indeed a watershed moment in your targeted job search campaign. It is a make or break opportunity to convince him to create a job for you (or find an existing job opening matching your ksa's). However, this is not the moment to revert to the standard interview tactics practiced by job seekers in the traditional job search: keep in mind that the majority of job seekers are wired to be interviewees – not interviewers. **Interviewers assume the role of talent experts in the position to do the assessments, evaluations, and decision-making.** Interviewees assume the role of job beggars who must pass certain exams with the right scores, and answer specific questions with the correct responses. To escape this vicious cycle, job seekers have to become excellent in a combination of two strategies: 1) pitching; 2) interviewing. Interviewing can be further defined in two ways: 1) being interviewed for someone else's pleasure; 2) being the interviewer for your pleasure.

When you are being interviewed by someone else, you **surrender control of your career brand to that person's subjective analysis of your responses.** In effect, you become a passive actor in someone else's script: a job posting or their imagination of a job's requirements. In the corporate recruitment process, you spend most of your time playing defense by simply using prepared responses to standard questions. As such, you will be judged against a standard you can't possibly know or imitate. Your career brand is designed to appeal to, and resonate with, specific audiences. Therefore, a large part of how you will be perceived will be based upon how closely aligned the interviewer is with your target audience. You will be up the creek without a paddle if you have the misfortune of being interviewed by company representatives who are unable to resonate with you. It's not as if you will be allowed to hand pick your interviewers like a trial lawyer picks members of a jury. Even if you make it to an interview with a Hiring Manager, there is no real cause for celebration: most Hiring Managers are hard-wired to follow the traditional interview script dictated by recruiters, and will instinctively attempt to interview you for their pleasure.

Instead of being a passive interviewee, an alternative is to be an active actor in a self-created script and interview for your pleasure – thus, becoming the interviewer. Using this strategy, you are able to ask the key questions needed to understand if the company is the best place for you to work – given the requirements of the job posting and workplace environment. It can be done through informational interviews prior to completing an online application or during the recruitment process if you are selected for an interview. This will put the recruiters and other stakeholders in the position of answering unscripted and meaningful questions about specific business challenges your role will be expected to tackle; thereby, enhancing your career brand. Unfortunately, job seekers who advance through formal recruitment processes have to be more concerned with answering structured interview questions from multiple interviewers than asking meaningful questions about the business. Interviewing is a necessary skill and is extremely useful when job seekers use it strategically to be an interviewer probing for knowledge rather than an interviewee being probed for incompetence. However, it is not the strategy of choice when speaking one-on-one with Hiring Managers. When you reach a Hiring Manager using the traditional or targeted job search, you will need to avoid falling prey to their basic instincts: conducting traditional interviews.

"Prepare talking points and practice delivering them, whether you have 10 seconds for an elevator pitch, 60 seconds for a commercial or 10 minutes for an informational interview." – www.career-advice.monster.com

Job seekers in the targeted job search conduct informational interviews with networking contacts to gather market intelligence on the most pressing challenges facing their target companies. In the case when you are proposing the creation of a new job tailored to your ksa's, a traditional interview with a Hiring Manager simply won't cut it. You will need to develop superb skills at pitching for projects, in addition to interviewing for jobs. Pitching is the art of presenting something of professed usefulness to someone who you believe will derive value from it. **Pitching puts you in control of the discussion and allows you to customize your message for the Hiring Manager's pressing needs** (which you uncovered through market intelligence gathered from informational interviews and job postings). When you get the opportunity to speak with a Hiring Manager, it is extremely important that it is not wasted on a traditional interview. It can be argued (and rightfully so) that even a traditional interview with a Hiring Manager is highly preferable to a traditional interview with a recruiter. But the fact is it's still an interview that can fall prey to an interviewer's biases, and proclivity to ask structured questions that have little to do with your ability to address specific business challenges. When you pitch for projects, you present solutions to identified challenges the company is currently facing or will be facing in the near future.

When you interview for jobs, you are only presenting questions that, however intelligent they may be, are still just questions. **Questions only raise issues, but pitches offer solutions.** Asking questions is for your pleasure, but pitching solutions is for the Hiring Manager's pleasure. And since a professional service provider-oriented job seeker is in the business of client satisfaction, it is the pleasure of the Hiring Manager that is of utmost importance. Pitching for projects gives you the opportunity to position yourself in accordance with your career brand and what you do best. It's your opportunity to create a job that doesn't exist – one tailored to your unique skillset. Companies can't design every possible job they will need to tackle their challenges, so it is up to you to pitch an opportunity that creates a job for yourself: in effect, ensuring you have no competition from other job seekers. Job seekers being funneled through the formal recruitment process will never be afforded an opportunity to commandeer an interviewer's time to make a project pitch. The best they will be able to muster up is a forced two-minute pitch that will only register as a stale response to the interview question: *Why should I hire you?*

"Many a worthwhile project has gotten the thumbs-down because it wasn't pitched effectively. Before you delve into your rehearsed spiel on why your project demands the green light, make sure it hits the ears of the right person at the right time." – www.techrepublic.com

If pitching for projects were easy, then every job seeker would do it. However, the average job seeker is resigned to interviewing for the jobs which companies "copy and paste" on the job boards. Whether you reach the Hiring Manager using the traditional or targeted search, the ability to pitch for projects will likely land you a job over your interview-only counterparts. Job seekers who have followed the preceding steps of the targeted job search are in a much better position to pitch for projects because their entire objective was designed for that purpose. It is similar to the difference between a professor who researches business strategies versus a professional who creates business strategies. There are many tactics to deliver successful pitches and they will all depend upon your subject matter expertise, target companies, and profile of the Hiring Managers. However, you can generally group the art of pitching for projects into two strategies.

1. **Formal Pitching.** If you are lucky enough to get a scheduled meeting with a Hiring Manager, then you will have the luxury of preparing a formal pitch. It is to your advantage when you know the location and time you'll spend with a Hiring Manager. This allows you to plan your pitch according to the

location's infrastructure and to know how long the pitch should be. It also gives you the assurance that you'll be able to discuss the main solutions that are most important to the business. Whereas most interviewers are concerned with what you've done in the past, you will have to convince a Hiring Manager to be more focused on what you can do in the present (and future). This is the "show and tell" moment that puts you in the position of being a resource person rather than a job beggar.

2. **Informal Pitching.** Sometimes a meeting with a Hiring Manager takes place over lunch, at a conference, or during a leisure-time activity. Your ability to persuasively communicate your value proposition will be the deciding factor on whether or not you get hired. In some cases, this is preferable depending on your communications style and the particular nature of what you are pitching. Think of how politicians, religious leaders, and television personalities persuade people to take action by appealing to their values and challenges. Time is a factor that will be out of your control during an informal pitch: be prepared to make the key elements of your pitch in a few minutes or less. Oftentimes, this informal interplay can lead to an invitation with a Hiring Manager where you will be able to use the formal pitching strategy.

Former Chrysler CEO, Lee Iacocca, once said, *"You can have brilliant ideas, but if you can't get them across, your ideas won't get you anywhere."* At the heart of pitching for projects is the ability to get brilliant solutions across to a Hiring Manager. Your pitch will carry more weight if you are introduced via a personal endorsement from a Trusted Source. Though it is possible for job seekers to pitch to Hiring Managers in the formal recruitment process, the chances of it happening are slim given the nature of the structured interviews: you will find yourself on the receiving end of standard interview questions with little time left to actually pitch why you are the best person for the job. When you have an audience with a Hiring Manager, it will be up to you to clearly state the objectives of the meeting (in the case of a formal pitch) in order to ensure that your well-planned pitch does not turn into the average interview for a job. Think of yourself as a salesperson meeting a prospective client to present your product's features and benefits that will remove, or greatly reduce, a source of pain felt by her company.

"And before you approach that person (the Hiring Manager), you should be familiar with what he or she considers his or her biggest pain point to be. Obviously, your project should make his or her life easier. If not, your suggestion will quickly be forgotten." – www.techrepublic.com

Chapter 24
Negotiated Employment Offer Versus Standard Employment Offer

"During a negotiation, it would be wise not to take anything personally. If you leave personalities out of it, you will be able to see opportunities more objectively." – Brian Koslow

Your employment offer is always the stickiest subject to be discussed with the Hiring Manager. But it is indeed the Hiring Manager you want to be having this conversation with – not a recruiter! Job seekers in the formal recruitment process won't be able to escape the meddling of a recruiter who is only concerned with standardizing employment offers. However, when you bypass recruiters and pitch yourself directly to a Hiring Manager, you will be able to control the standards by which you will be compensated. A company's philosophy to employment offers boils down to two schools of thought: 1) pay for time; 2) pay for deliverable. Most companies have a standard employment offer based on your working a standard number of hours within a work-week (40 hours – plus or minus five – for most industrialized countries). However, **as a corporate employee you are trapped in a confusing definition of compensation because you are not expressly paid for your time or your deliverables.** That means your base salary won't change regardless of any extra hours you work or the value of your contributions to the company. This is not a bad deal if you're an average corporate employee, but it is highway robbery if you're a high-potential employee putting in extra hours while simultaneously making huge contributions to the bottom line. A standard employment offer is not designed to value your individual talents and abilities. It is designed based on a predefined value for job functions within the company.

"Genentech offers competitive salaries that vary by department, job function and experience. Our salary guidelines are reviewed annually to ensure that they are competitive within the industry." – Genentech

More often than not, **companies will seek to place you within the lower to middle range of salary bands that are linked with certain job functions and titles.** The salary bands at most global corporations are usually determined by the big four HR consultancies (Aon Hewitt, Hay Group, Mercer, and Towers Watson) that do global salary benchmarking surveys and analysis for large, multinational corporations. If you go through the corporate recruiting process then you will always receive the standard employment offer with little room to improve it. You will be confined to the predetermined value of the job for which you applied. Depending on your target companies' compensation philosophy, the standard employment offer can fall below expectations or it can exceed expectations. The probability is high that it will fall below in a buyer's (employers) market and exceed in a seller's (job seekers) market. Regardless of where the needle falls on the standard employment offer scale, you should not take it at face value. Outside of the formal recruitment process, job seekers have more flexibility to negotiate an employment offer to meet their specific needs as well as those of the Hiring Manager's. This is only possible because you won't have to deal with recruiters and HR staff whose mission is to confine your compensation value to what they feel is appropriate. Whereas the standard employment offer treats you like a "me too" product that is priced the same as the next carbon copy, the negotiated employment offer allows you to get some extra value for the unique features and benefits you can provide.

"You would discuss the specifics of the salary for each position with the Human Resources representative or hiring manager. Our compensation and benefits plans are based on national benchmarking studies to ensure that they are competitive. Our salaries are based on the market value of the position and take into consideration an applicant's experience and education." – 3M

It is wise to negotiate your employment offer directly with the Hiring Manager – not with the corporate recruiter. Some Hiring Managers will extend you an employment offer and then leave it to the corporate recruiter to handle the administrative details regarding salary and benefits. Do not let this happen to you! It is your responsibility to close the deal with the Hiring Manager regarding all financial and non-financial terms of your total compensation package – and get it in writing! This is the secret to how some job seekers get compensated better than their peers with similar backgrounds. When dealing directly with Hiring Managers, you are in a position to create a job for yourself versus just accepting an existing job. It is highly unlikely that a corporate recruiter will have the authority – or inclination – to create a job for you regardless of how much you could benefit his company. The benefit of creating a job gives you the advantage of assigning it a value based on what you are uniquely able to do. If the Hiring Manager is convinced by your project pitch, then he will be more likely to create a job for you at a negotiable compensation. Of course, this entails him negotiating with the Human Resources department; however, he is far better positioned to fight that battle than you are. Negotiating an employment offer with the Hiring Manager allows you to calculate the value of the unique solutions you are able to provide to the company: those that directly affect the bottom line.

In major professional sports, the players who are able to contribute more than the average players will be the ones who are compensated accordingly. In the corporate world, imagine if Mark Zuckerberg had finished college and applied online to be an employee at IBM. It's reasonable to say that he would have received a standard employment offer. Although I'm sure that offer would have been above average, the fact is that IBM would never have valued him for his entrepreneurial and visionary talents. The negotiated employment offer allows you to define the terms of the employment arrangement, whereas the standard employment offer implies a standard workweek according to the company's definition for exempt employees. Companies always need talented workers who can bring value by making them money or saving them money. Yet, you will find that many companies do not want to hire fulltime employees outside of the job postings they have advertised. This is where dealing directly with the Hiring Manager allows you to target a company's needs – instead of its job postings. **Targeting a company's needs always** opens the door for you to create a job while targeting its job postings only opens the door for you to apply online.

"In most companies hiring managers make decisions about how to allocate their budgets. Generally HR representatives are messengers who report your past salary, salary requirements etc to the hiring manager. In some organizations the HR manager negotiates on behalf of the hiring manager. Find out who makes the final decision about salary and perks and, if possible, deal directly with that person." – www.jobdig.com

By targeting the company's needs – more specifically the Hiring Manager's needs – you can negotiate an offer to work as a freelancer or contractor for a specified value: effectively bypassing any fulltime hiring constraints the company may have. In order to be compensated in line with the value you can bring to your target companies, you'll have to be clear on the value of the solutions you can provide those companies. You'll also need to assign a financial value to the non-financial metrics that impact a company's bottom line. Final warning: when discussing compensation, be sure to never ever speak with a recruiter or anyone else in Human Resources. HR is programmed to follow policy and practice regarding compensation and will try to measure you against the salary bands of their average corporate employees. This certainly doesn't do you any good if you want your unique skillset to be valued for its actual worth. Only the Hiring Manager is in a position to evaluate your worth to her department, business unit, and company: assuming you are dealing with the competent, business-minded sort. With regard to the Hiring Manager, there are three methods you can use to negotiate an employment offer.

1. **Contract Offer Based On Deliverable.** You can negotiate an employment offer based on an agreed-upon project deliverable. The compensation you receive will be determined by the value of the project you deliver. However, for this contract to work it is paramount that you know what resources will be made available to you before agreeing a price. This contract is suitable for Hiring Managers that want to know exactly what they will get for the compensation you

receive. How you structure your compensation is negotiable, and this gives you the flexibility to incorporate both financial and non-financial payments. For deliverables-based projects, the amount of hours you work is irrelevant since your compensation is a function of the successful completion of the project by an agreed deadline – not the hours spent on it.

2. **Contract Offer Based On Time.** If you negotiate an employment offer based on time, then you'll need to estimate the number of hours it will take you to complete an agreed-upon project. This means you should have an hourly and daily rate for your services, in addition to other non-financial payments you will accept. You'll also need to be clear on the entire scope of the project and the resources you'll have at your disposal. This type of contract works best when the parameters of the project are clearly stated, and a Hiring Manager can pay for your services on an hourly basis until the project is complete. For time-based projects, the amount of hours you work are relevant to the compensation you will receive to deliver the project by an agreed deadline.

3. **Fulltime Offer Based On Contribution.** You always have the option to negotiate a fulltime job offer if it is your goal. However, don't fall prey to the standard employment offer trap that lets the Hiring Manager randomly assign your compensation based on what is paid to other employees. Once you determine the value of your contribution to the company's bottom line, you'll have an easier time convincing the Hiring Manager that you merit any additional compensation you are worth. However, there is one catch: you'll need to negotiate having a job created for you so that the Hiring Manager and HR department can justify the additional compensation. Why? Because most companies are still based on old models of compensation that value years of experience over ingenuity, and job titles over job contribution.

Getting hired is only part of the equation when pitching directly to a Hiring Manager; the other part is getting properly compensated. When you use the right negotiation techniques, it opens a range of possibilities for companies to compensate you appropriately. When discussing compensation, I am describing both financial and non-financial payments that are tradable for your knowledge, skills, and abilities. The balance between financial and non-financial compensation must be carefully considered: with special attention given to the non-financial components. Companies oftentimes have more flexibility to negotiate the non-financials and this increases the probability of closing a mutually beneficial agreement. It is up to you to negotiate the best employment offer for yourself because the Hiring Manager most certainly will not do it for you. Dealing directly with Hiring Managers is the only way you can have a business-to-business conversation regarding your impact on the company's bottom line. Most competent Hiring Managers are accustomed to negotiating business deals that bring the best possible value to their companies. For this reason, presenting yourself as Me Inc. will allow you to sell yourself as a business opportunity that will benefit the company. **It is up to you to make clear the value of your features and benefits that will compel the Hiring Manager to say:** *"You're hired!"*

Chapter 25
Summary: Journey To The Hiring Manager

"Two roads diverged in a wood, and I, I took the one less traveled by, and that has made all the difference." – Robert Frost

The targeted job search puts you in control of your job search and career decisions instead of relying on a recruiter in the corporate recruitment process to make those decisions for you. By building your career brand and networking strategically, you will be able to find alternative paths to reach the Hiring Managers at your target companies. **There are always more ways to get to the Hiring Manager besides the one-way path that is the corporate recruitment process.** Using the targeted job search obliges you to take an entrepreneurial approach to managing your career objectives. It relies on your ability to be a self-starter and to behave as a responsible business entity. When you are trying to convince a Hiring Manager to hire you, it will have to be based on more than just the eye candy of a traditional résumé, and ear candy of a formal interview. While those tools may be standard protocol for the traditional job search, they won't be nearly as effective in the targeted job search. Few job seekers use the targeted job search because it is a more demanding process that requires:

1. **Self-Confidence.** Being self-aware and knowing how the aggregate of your personal and professional qualities form a unique value proposition that will benefit companies experiencing myriad challenges.

2. **Business Acumen.** Going beyond merely having knowledge of business concepts, and knowing how you can uniquely apply those concepts to the benefit of your target companies.

3. **Unrelenting Perseverance.** Overcoming roadblocks you encounter by developing innovative ways to overcome them and having the discipline to stay the course until you locate

the right people who will value what you can do for their business.

The targeted job search is a self-created recruitment process that creates myriad possibilities to get hired. This is in direct contrast to the corporate recruitment process that is linear and beset with lock-step stages controlled by the recruiter. In the targeted job search, your imagination and creativity will determine your success in getting a job – not the whim of a recruiter. There are some essential strategies for you to embrace that will facilitate your journey that are not easy to commit to (which is why the majority of job seekers choose to suffer in online application hell). While online applications allow for a quick submission process to mass numbers of companies, it is the method that is least successful in getting extended an employment offer. Don't be a job seeker who simply accepts that following the rules of the corporate recruitment process is the only way to get hired. Be a rules breaker and blaze your own trail! At best, you'll take control over your own job placement – assuming you have something of value to offer an employer. At worst, you'll at least be more prepared to differentiate yourself among the job seekers corralled in the corporate recruitment process.

"Remember that there are thousands of people out there looking for work, and this kind of targeted job search takes time and effort. So do not waste your time with building relationships with people and companies you do not want to work for! Instead, focus on your chosen companies – the companies you researched and know will offer you the best possible career opportunity. That way you are more likely to secure a job that you would be happy to keep for a period time that fits your particular career aspirations." – www.thedailyrecuiter.com

Many job seekers are tempted to take the path of least resistance when applying online. But this plays right into the hands of a corporate recruitment game that is designed to confuse and manipulate you – unless you fit the desired mold of either a corporate drone or a corporate promotable. When you conduct the targeted job search, it is like using the "Sword Of Omens": it will give you sight beyond sight, and allow you to see through the employer branding-infused mirages in the game. At every turn, you will encounter Corporate Agents who will attempt to thwart your progress. They cannot be reasoned with, or convinced to assist you in your journey to the Hiring Manager: therefore, you must identify them before they identify you and avoid engagement at all costs. Corporate Agents only desire to turn you into fodder for the ATS. While traditional job seekers charge full speed ahead into the alligator-filled moat surrounding the stronghold of the corporate recruiters; the targeted job seekers use a catapult to propel themselves over it and directly into the center of the Hiring Managers' chambers. Once there, they enjoy the spoils of having exclusive access to the real decision makers. However, it is important to remember that gaining access is only half the battle: the other half is having something of substance to say. If you conduct a half-hearted targeted job search, then you will get half-hearted results.

"During your targeted job search do not be tempted to blindly send in your resume to the companies HR department. This would constitute a total waste of time as a letter addressed to no one will indeed be opened by no one. Get the name and contact details of the actual hiring manager, as this will be the person you most want to communicate your skills and level of interest in the position with!" – www.thedailyrecruiter.com

I don't want to give the illusion that the targeted job search is a panacea that will work for you 100% of the time. No process is that effective. What I do want to impress upon you is that using the targeted job search will make you smarter, and add more value to your career brand throughout the duration of your job search campaign and professional career. The research you conduct on job postings from various companies to collect market intelligence on your areas of expertise will ensure that you maintain and develop the skills that are in demand. Using your mind to constantly innovate ways to reach your target companies will open doors that you otherwise might never have opened. Each day of your job search will add a little more to your unique value proposition that can be directly translated into how well you will impact business results. Instead of being glossy-eyed over employer branding campaigns enticing you to apply online, you can decide which companies it makes sense for you to pursue based on objective research. The targeted job search obliges you to judge target companies based on the metrics you deem important instead of those dictated by the corporate recruiters. And it obliges you to deliver your business solutions directly to a Hiring Manager instead of wasting time trying to get past gatekeeping recruiters.

Level Four

Global Corporations Do The Deceiving

Chapter 26
Globally Ranked Employers

"Choosing an employer after college is an intensely personal process. A company that's perfect for one job seeker may be perfectly wrong for another. But even if priorities differ, all job seekers care about many of the same things: pay and promotions, corporate culture, and training programs, to name a few." – www.businessweek.com

The companies ranked as ideal employers and best places to work are not always deserving of those rankings. They are indeed the masters of the corporate recruitment game and use every trick in the book to keep you playing. Their genius is in convincing you that they are not the villains in the game. They hide behind dubious rankings and awards on the one hand, while treating job seekers like cannon fodder on the other. You only need to do some basic research on how these employers have treated their workforce to find the wolves in sheeps' clothing. Companies polish their image as employers of choice through employer branding (EB) campaigns just as they use product branding to create a positive image of their products – even when those products do not perform as advertised. EB has taken on greater importance to Human Resources departments over the past several years as talented job seekers exercise greater discretion in choosing their future employers. Each year, EB campaigns evolve to keep the best and the brightest potential employees actively applying online instead of contacting Hiring Managers directly, or starting their own companies.

"The results of the American Student Survey reveal how students perceive organizations as employers in the United States. The research functions as a basis for decision-making when choosing target groups, messages and channels for future employer branding campaigns, and as a control instrument for measuring the appeal an organization has over its specific target groups." – www.universumglobal.com

While there is no standard accepted definition for what constitutes a good employer brand, the only way you should define it is by how a company's employer value proposition (EVP) – made up of its policies, practices, profitability, and people – will affect your ability to perform at a high level. Very few job seekers look behind the numbers of the globally ranked employers to ascertain what goes on behind the scenes. An employer's ranking, no matter how prestigious the rankings publication, is not a proxy for EVP. However, many job seekers flock to these employer rankings publications to choose their target employers in the same way that prospective students flock to the business school rankings publications sold by Businessweek and Financial Times that purport to rank the world's best MBA programs. An employer rankings publication does not make an employer of choice; the satisfaction and engagement of employees do. Yet, job seekers are made to believe (through EBHP) that employer rankings publications are *pseudo* regulatory agencies tasked with protecting the interests of job seekers against unprincipled employers. Consequently, companies have free reign to continue exaggerating claims about their EVP on websites, at presentations, and during interviews without providing any objective metrics to support them. The average job seeker takes the employer branding bait like the cheese in a mousetrap, and the best EB campaigns ensure that you never question anything that is contrary to what the company would have you believe.

Companies ranked as employers of choice should have a moral and legal obligation to provide greater EVP transparency to job seekers – but they have neither. There is no regulatory agency governing the transparency and veracity of the statements companies make about their EVP. There is no consumer protection agency to regulate companies' EB campaigns. Indeed, there is no existing entity that can compel global employers to provide you with investor-grade EVP transparency. Therefore, don't hold your breath waiting for them to voluntarily make this information available for your pleasure. There will not be an EVP Prospectus or EVP Annual Report for you. This is all part and parcel of the corporate recruitment game that propagates the business practice of hoodwinking jobseekers into playing a game of shadows: with you being the one chasing the shadows of the

EVP you thought existed. The companies ranked as employers of choice have no incentive to damage their employer brands by providing unflattering metrics about themselves. Job seekers will rarely find companies that produce transparent metrics that objectively measure the statements on their websites or those made during the recruitment process. Employers can't control the recruitment game to their advantage if you start making informed decisions based on objective data instead of the plethora of subjective data they feed you. Therefore, it is not in their best interests to help you to become a wiser job seeker.

Most companies do not – and will not – provide measurable data that corroborates their "sales" pitch to potential employees as a great place to work. While external surveys that measure an employer brand are useful for a company, they do not provide any useful data for you to analyze. The rankings publications do not make publicly available the raw data used to calculate the employer rankings. At best, they only tell you the dimensions that they evaluate and the weightings assigned to those dimensions. It will be a rarity to find the actual survey questions given to employees and the actual number of employees participating in the survey. In the end, employer rankings publications provide you with little insight and virtually no objective EVP data. However, they do sell magazines for publishers and give employers great ammunition for EB campaigns. So at least someone is benefitting from all of this hoopla – just not you. The top ranked companies skillfully use EB to avoid being transparent about their EVP. Not surprising since that is what most marketing and advertising campaigns are designed to do. **Companies are far more transparent in their Annual Reports than they are in their Workplace Reports.** Potential investors have loads of quantitative data to pore over: replete with plans and strategies to address pending challenges and future aspirations. But the same does not hold true for potential employees seeking the best workplace environments in which to invest their knowledge, skills, and abilities.

"Best Companies for Leadership are at the forefront of a major shift. They are moving away from traditional structures where direction comes from on high, via a strict hierarchy." – www.haygroup.com

Today's social media explosion gives companies more ways in which to cast a wider EB net. Social media tools are not used by these companies for the purpose of engaging job seekers in any meaningful two-way communications. Quite the contrary! The globally ranked employers merely use these tools to further cement their façade as employers of choice. Their ability to engage in questionable EB practices and shady recruitment games has been magnified by the network effects of social media. It has never been easier for job seekers to do thorough background checks on companies by using various social media platforms (LinkedIn, Facebook, etc.) and reading online employer reviews (Glassdoor, Vault, Jobitorial, etc.). But global employers are adapting by also using social media platforms to counteract any negative press they receive. This phenomenon makes it more difficult (but not impossible) to discern the truly best places to work from the EB-drenched fakes. You will need to learn how to judge an employer against objective data according to the criteria you believe makes a great place to work. Of course, globally-ranked employers won't make it easy for you to expose their charade: they didn't achieve their global rankings by playing by the rules – they created the rules.

It is not easy to resist the temptation of believing that a globally-ranked employer of choice offers a great employer value proposition. Even though most of the EB campaigns you are exposed to only serve to create a corporate fairytale, your mind makes it real because of your desire to be a corporate employee and to obtain all of the associated accoutrements. In many ways these companies are like casino houses because no matter how many times you lose at the table, they convince you that it is worth it to continue playing the game. Casinos provide free alcoholic beverages to keep gamblers sufficiently inebriated in order to encourage them to continue spending money on games they will rarely win. If everyone thought rationally and contemplated the probabilities of actually hitting the jackpot, then casino houses would go bankrupt. The same is true in the corporate recruitment game. EB campaigns (employer branding hocus pocus) are the free alcohol, and applying online is the compulsive gambling on dealer-controlled games. As long as major corporations have databases full of job applicants, they are less inclined to radically change the raw deal they give you as a job seeker. But if there ever comes a day when the top job seekers stop playing the game, the jig will be up for these so-called "employers of choice".

"Based on the preferences of over 160,000 career seekers, with a business or engineering background from the world´s 12 largest economies (based on nominal GDP), Universum releases the global talent attraction index: The World's Most Attractive Employers 2011." – www.universumglobal.com

Chapter 27
Judging An Employer By Its Cover

"It is precisely the purpose of the public opinion generated by the press to make the public incapable of judging, to insinuate into it the attitude of someone irresponsible, uninformed." – Walter Benjamin

As a job seeker, companies are constantly judging you by your cover. When you network with potential employer contacts, they will make judgments about your organizational fit based on how you communicate (physical, verbal, and written). When you attend company presentations, they will make judgments based on your perceived interest and the quality of your questions. When you apply online to a job posting, they will make judgments based on the presentation and quality of your application materials. When you complete a pre-interview assessment test, they will make judgments of your aptitude based on your scores. And finally, **when companies google your name, they will make judgments based on your social media footprint – or lack thereof.** Is this fair? Probably not. Is this reality? Absolutely! The game is designed as such but you are told otherwise. Corporate recruiters would have you believe that the game is fair and that you are judged by the content of your application, not the appearance of your Facebook profile. Do not fall for that trap! You can be excluded from the recruitment process because of a controversial Facebook profile if the recruiter deems it out of character with the company's image. Of course, few recruiters will publicly acknowledge that and none will inform you when it happens.

"Submit your résumé/CV. Our recruiters will review it, and if we find opportunities that match your interests, we'll contact you to set up an initial interview." – Cemex

The adage, *"don't judge a book by its cover"*, doesn't seem to apply during the recruitment process. Before you are even granted an opportunity to interview for a job, the company will have already formed an opinion about your professional brand

and fit within its organization based upon both qualitative and quantitative assessments. Likewise, you should be judging an employer by its cover. Whether you use the traditional job search or the targeted job search, you need to make some basic judgments about the companies for which you desire to work before you begin applying to their job postings, or pitching projects to their Hiring Managers. **You need to judge whether a company's workplace is conducive for your unique knowledge, skills, and abilities.** Given the importance of the job search process and investment of your time, it is essential to answer some key questions about your target companies' EVP. Be advised: companies are not very forthcoming with this information. You'll need to use a combination of a company's website, employer review sites, and networking (online and offline) in order to make a sound judgment that satisfies your concerns. **The information age has not only made it easier for consumers to judge product brands before they buy, but also for job seekers to judge employer brands before they apply.**

So where do you begin when deciding how to judge an employer? As Steven Covey said, *"begin with the end in mind"*, and that end is the workplace environment itself because the purpose of your job search campaign is to get hired. You will need to gather data that measure a company's EVP as it is promoted by its EB campaigns. Your performance and satisfaction with any employer will depend on how closely aligned you are with its EVP. I've identified 12 EVP components that I believe are the best way to validate whether or not an employer is worthy of your consideration and the time investment it will take to pursue an employment opportunity. The level of importance and the degree to which you assess each component will depend upon your personal and professional expectations. The more objective data you are able to gather to answer your key employment concerns, the better the position you'll be in to know whether or not a prospective employer's EB pitch is all smoke and mirrors. One look at online job postings and corporate downsizing reports lets you know that employers are well practiced in the art of "bait and switch" advertising. Therefore, you should not let yourself be too easily fooled by crafty words and toothless babble.

"Brocade encourages and rewards fresh ideas, bold decisions, and professional growth. Brocade employees feel energized by the work they do, the people they work with and the impact they make. These are just a few of the reasons why Brocade continues to grow faster than other companies and why it is ranked as a top employer of choice." – Brocade

"A career at The Coca-Cola Company is truly a one-of-a-kind experience. It's more than working for the global beverage leader; it's an opportunity to be a part of something that impacts the world. From our product portfolio to the planet itself, we offer you not only the chance to build a successful career -- we offer you an opportunity to make a difference in the world." – Coca-Cola

Many companies do not take stock of all the components constituting their EVP. They offer little in terms of detailed data to support the very employer brand they claim to have – other than fabrications of a workplace utopia. Having a job that is perfectly aligned to your career brand will be meaningless if the EVP is not also aligned. The level to which you are able to integrate within the company's workplace environment will affect the success you are able to sustain. In the ensuing chapters, you will learn how the 12 EVP components are essential to your capacity to objectively judge employers as best places to work. It is essential to have an idea of what an employer values and how transparent it is with metrics that support its candidacy as an employer of choice. There are plenty of questions you could formulate for each of the 12 components. However, it is more important to focus on analyzing the data you are most likely to find. Since companies are not legally bound to make publicly available the details of their EVP, it is highly unlikely that you will be able to get all the answers you want before becoming an employee. And that is what the purveyors of the corporate recruitment game are counting on.

The game is fueled by the ignorance and complacency of job seekers. Their desire to become corporate employees makes it easy for the game to cajole them into jobs that are not the best fit for their ksa's. Regardless of the job search method you choose to become a corporate employee, you will still need to use objective criteria to judge the employers for which you want to work. Failure to judge an employer objectively could derail your career before it even starts. Do not rely on corporate recruiters, Corporate Agents, and Hiring Managers to air the company's dirty laundry. They will always put the company's ethics ahead of their own moral obligations to be transparent and truthful with information that could be important to your career management. Their deception will have no limits, and any request for full disclosure will be blocked at every turn. They will practice omission-of-details in their employer branding campaigns instead of truth-in-advertising. Their mission is to build your thirst to be a corporate employee to a crescendo that only the completion of an online application can satiate. They would have you believe that you could most likely be *"The ONE"*, when in reality you will most likely be the one to get rejected by the recruitment process.

What's in it for you as a corporate employee? That is the question you will need to answer as you judge your target employers; more specifically, as you judge their employer value propositions. The genius of the corporate recruitment game is its effectiveness in keeping you busy jumping through myriad hoops to become a corporate employee instead of objectively judging the company's key EVP components. The very information that can aid your discovery process of a company's worthiness to be considered an employer of choice is not even made a centerpiece of the hiring process. This is not an accident or a mere oversight by *"the powers that be"* who manage the corporate recruitment game – this is by design. Companies do not want to be put under the microscope by the inquiring minds of savvy job seekers: they prefer to put you under instead. When you go through the formal recruitment process, companies will gather all the data they need to make a judgment about your employee value proposition. Any perceived flaws in your profile could lead to your dismissal from the process without even the dignity of a fair trial: don't expect corporate recruiters and Hiring Managers to be impartial judges. Avoiding the formal recruitment process does not excuse you from doing your due diligence to judge your target employers' EVP. Not only will this information help you to formulate a sound strategy to get hired, but more importantly, it will lay bare the EVP hazards for which you will need to formulate a career management strategy during your employment tenure.

Chapter 28
EVP Component #1: Job Posting Advertisements (JPA)

"They don't have enough information. They are written purposely to mislead you, because the "employer" wants to hide from you what the job really is; or to make you think there's a job when there isn't." – www.jobwatch.org.au

No job seeker should accept at face value what is written on a job posting. It is always good practice to read the fine print – or lack thereof. Job postings are merely written characterizations of what an employee might do (or is expected to do) in a job position. They are oftentimes based on fantasy instead of reality, wishes instead of priorities, and tasks instead of results. They can be written by recruiters in direct collaboration with Hiring Managers, or written by Hiring Managers in collaboration with the co-workers who are stakeholders in the job position. In the worst case, the job postings are written solely by recruiters who have limited knowledge of the day-to-day roles and expectations of the jobs. **Since you will never know the true nature of the job until you actually become an employee, it is to your advantage to analyze what is written and clarify any questionable text by asking the appropriate questions.** It is as much a risk for you to pursue a poorly described job as it is for the company. Properly written job postings will clearly target specific job seekers, communicate specific challenges to be addressed, and provide insights into the company's workplace environment. JPA's are an essential tool used by employer branding campaigns designed to attract new and unsuspecting players to enter into the corporate recruitment game by applying online. They should always be viewed with suspicion, and carefully inspected to determine the level of EBHP contamination. In spite of the hazards presented by most JPA's, they are still great sources of market intelligence for job seekers who know how to scavenge them for useful tidbits.

"As you search the positions we have available, you'll have the opportunity to save jobs that interest you, apply for the position that best

matches your background and keep track of your application once you've submitted it." – *Pfizer*

1. **Judge The Clarity Of The Job Postings**

When looking at job postings, it's nearly impossible to understand the encoded messages embedded throughout the requirements, qualifications, responsibilities, preferences, and other miscellaneous information desired by the company. Unless you are a professional job seeker who knows which jobs to pass over and which ones to pursue, you'll more than likely fall prey to "applying and waiting" for myriad job postings. If you know how to interpret the JPA code, you'll be able to see that many job postings are written to discourage you from applying. A rule of thumb to follow is if the JPA seems overly descriptive and impossible for any normal human being to do, then it probably is. The JPA allows you to judge an employer's workplace flexibility, form, and function – if you can see past the advertising gimmicks. Like a word problem from a college entrance exam, JPA's oblige you to identify the superfluous and unnecessary text in order to decipher what is really being communicated.

Some JPA's focus on years of work experience, certifications, and preferred qualifications. The message here is that a standard corporate employee profile has already been decided and that any job seeker differing from that profile will be judged with suspicion (if at all!). On one extreme, these employers generally value seniority over ingenuity, stability over adaptability, rigidity over flexibility, conformity over individuality, and similarity over diversity. The reverse also holds true in that some postings are extremely flexible and non-descript. In that case, you may indeed value the reverse of the previously listed ordered pairs depending on your personality and values. In rare cases, you'll find well-written JPA's that emphasize the function of the job and describe the key performance indicators by which you'll be evaluated. These employers generally value smart, motivated, and results-oriented people who are able to perform a job that has a specific and measurable purpose.

2. **Judge The Value Of The Job Postings**

It is important that you assess the JPA for more than what is actually written on it. Many employers seem to have mastered the "Jedi Mind Trick" (a.k.a. Employer Branding Hocus Pocus) by making job seekers read more into the job posting than what is actually there. It won't even occur to you what was missing until after you become an employee and then you realize every concern you wish you had voiced prior to accepting the job. If you have something of value to offer an employer and are confident in your ability to deliver, then the last thing you want is to end up in a dead-end job. How many JPA's have you seen that actually list the key performance indicators (kpi's)? How many tell you the additional roles for which the job will prepare you? How about the contribution of the job to the department's (and company's) success? That type of information should be clearly stated on the JPA in order to determine the job's true worth to the company. Not only will this aid you in determining what your compensation package should be, but it will also allow you to determine if you are even the right person for the job.

The value of the JPA is not only something to be viewed in financial terms but also in emotional terms. If the job is vaguely described and loaded with dubious requirements, then how important is it really to the company? With that in mind, look for JPA's that are presented in a highly professional format with appealing content designed to attract the top job candidates. They will usually contain more details about the job, the team, the business unit, and the kpi's. This will at least give you an idea of the value an employer places on the job. What is not listed on the JPA will usually determine whether or not you should even pursue the job. For example, you won't find much data about the personality profile and management style of your prospective boss; whether or not the job is new or existing; what happened to the person previously holding the job; and the idiosyncrasies of the workplace environment. All of those things will have an emotional effect on how you would be able to perform the job and must be taken into consideration.

3. **Judge The Probability Of Feedback**

Customer service is a lost art in many aspects of business these days. It is taken to a new low by the way employers deal with job seekers who enter the formal recruitment process. You might think that after showing interest in JPA's and investing time to complete online applications, that companies would be inclined to treat you like a valued customer. You might even expect the common courtesy of timely feedback (or any feedback, for that matter!). Not surprisingly, employers continue to disappoint. Job seekers applying online should be afforded the respect given to customers who purchase the company's products. However, job seekers are oftentimes left stranded on an island throwing up smoke signals in hopes of getting a live response from a submitted application. After all, who has time to be bothered with pesky job seekers and applicants only seeking feedback for the very jobs posted by the company? Employers who provide the contact information for actual people managing their selection processes are ones likely to provide feedback on your application – or at least allow you to follow up with an inquiry.

It is all too easy to look at JPA's and assume you'll be contacted for an interview at best, or receive feedback on why you weren't contacted at worst. What you didn't count on was the fact that corporate recruiters rode the short bus to the training courses on client orientation and customer service. There should be no middle ground when it comes to corporate values: meaning that a company can't claim to value customer service for the purchasers of its products but not value customer service for the applicants of its jobs. If an employer provides no useable means to have a live conversation with a potential applicant, then that doesn't bode well for the probability that you'll receive any feedback on a submitted job application. Beware the most egregious trick that is used by recruiters when a JPA looks too good to be true: they are oftentimes already filled by an internal candidate, or a job seeker who pursued a self-created process and had the job designed specifically for him. These jobs will be the ones that are described in great detail and will list statements such as: *"Only candidates meeting the minimum requirements will be contacted"* and *"preferred qualifications"*.

Chapter 29
EVP Component #2: Career Site Communications (CSC)

"Corporate career sites have never been compelling enough to capture an audience. Despite huge advances in content management, content aggregation/curation, and content sharing, most sites remain little more than a thin veil for the ATS-delivered online application." – www.ere.net

It's become fashionable for companies to jazz up their career sites with video and social media tools. They are indeed the "point of sale" between the job seeker and the employer – at least they should be. **Don't expect to find any interactive, live communications with someone who could assist your job candidacy.** More often than not, you will only come away with more questions than answers after perusing the useless information provided by the company. You will rarely find metrics-based information detailing the EVP in terms of training and development, diversity and inclusion, and compensation and benefits. This information represents some of the most valuable assets a company has to offer in terms of its EVP. Therefore, you can be sure that the transparent details you want are not made public. They are under heavy security and guarded at all times by the Human Resources department and Corporate Agents. The best way to judge these companies is to focus on the information they don't provide you – which is usually the most important! The CSC's of many companies consists of general details regarding their EVP and many are increasingly listing more detailed career information inside their Sustainability Reports (Corporate Social Responsibility and Citizenship Reports). The companies that provide the most meaningful metrics will be the ones that understand that it is increasingly difficult to fool the top job seekers with EBHP. The CSC's that offer neither general details nor quantifiable data clearly communicate that the companies don't have much value for it, nor care that you do.

"poweRBrands is RB's marketing and sales game. To be a winner you need to use your innovative sales skills and marketing ideas to

outperform your rivals, and work your way up to be President of the company. To speed your journey to the top, you need to think and act like an RB person. You'll have fun and learn something new about life at a global FMCG along the way." – Reckitt-Benckiser

1. **Judge The Career Site's Target Audience And Available Information**

    Many CSC's are clearly designed to resonate with a specific job seeker demographic. It may come as a shock to your ego if you are not among the "desired" demographic but don't let pride cause you to ignore the obvious signs. Don't assume it was just an oversight by the employer for not including certain information that would appeal to you. Stop making excuses for companies that employ highly-paid experts in marketing, communications, and talent management! You don't see these same companies making oversights on advertising campaigns and information they make available for the products they sell, do you? If a CSC doesn't appeal to your professional needs, then it is because you are not part of the employer's target audience. It's a hard pill to swallow for the majority of job seekers: this is why there are more unqualified applications submitted to companies than necessary. Nevertheless, you must pay careful attention to the segmentation of the career site menu. Observe which job seeker demographics are targeted, and the relevance of the information provided about the EVP for those demographics. That will tell you a lot about the employer's recruitment focus, and whether or not you fall into the category of a "desirable candidate".

    Most CSC's won't provide any information of substance regarding EVP: meaning you should hold in high regard the few that do. If the information you are searching for on a career site is difficult to find, then that is because the employer has done so purposely. You don't see companies hiding the accolades they receive for being named an *"Ideal Employer"* and *"Great Place To Work"*, do you? When you find pertinent CSC's buried in the pages of the Annual Report or Sustainability Report, then that is usually not a good sign. In the majority of cases, hyperlinks will not be provided from the most salient pages on the career site that would allow you to jump directly to EVP statistics buried within 100-page plus reports. These employers operate under the assumption that you have all the time in the world to peruse every page on their career site. Customer-orientation as it pertains to job seekers is practically non-existent. In contrast, the communications on the website of BMW are designed to sell high-value automobiles to targeted demographics. Corporate recruiters should be trained to design CSC's that sell a high-value product (the EVP) to targeted job applicants. At least then you would be provided with all the relevant and important information needed to make the right career decision.

2. **Judge The Social Media Tools Available To Engage Job Seekers**

Don't be fooled by the lack (or ubiquity) of social media tools in a CSC arsenal. You'll find many career sites that are awash with all the major social media tools promoting their EVP, but what you won't find is any respectable level of personal engagement with a live stakeholder in the hiring process. Companies skilled in the art of EBHP will show their employees blogging, tweeting, podcasting, and gaming; however, rarely will you find a knowledgeable person who is involved directly in talent selection available on social media to have a two-way conversation with you. Even the interactive social media games favored by a growing number of companies do not get you any closer to speaking to a competent stakeholder. You should be looking for companies that are using the social media tools on their websites to engage you in the same way they engage the customers who purchase their products and services. Job seekers also make a "purchasing" transaction when they submit an application in exchange for the opportunity to be considered a job candidate.

Companies that are customer service oriented are increasingly using virtual customer service representatives to engage in live chat sessions while you peruse the offerings on their websites. Why this level of customer service is barely used in the recruitment process at global corporations is beyond comprehension. Recruiters are tasked with engaging potential employees just as salespersons are tasked with engaging potential buyers. What message does an employer send when it doesn't provide you any means to communicate openly with it before you decide to complete an application? Especially given all the advances in social media technology that make it easier than ever to engage job seekers – with virtually no cost to either the company or job seeker! There is no excuse for employers not to make it standard practice to facilitate two-way communications via social media with job seekers before obliging them to complete an online application. However, when it concerns social media on the CSC's, you will find that many companies only use it to promote featured JPA's, facilitate JPA sharing, link to JPA search pages, and login to ATS's.

Chapter 30
EVP Component #3: Selection And Hiring Strategies (SAH)

"We've tried to make the application process as quick and easy as possible. But it's still worth investing time and energy in preparing your application. A strong, considered application can make a difference." – BP

Most job seekers face the unenviable task of applying online to numerous job postings and then waiting for responses – usually not favorable ones. For all the time you spend applying online, the one thing you will never know is who actually gets hired and how they got hired. **You'll have better luck finding a leprechaun than finding any detailed information on the number of hires sourced through a company's various recruitment channels.** The majority of companies lack transparency in providing SAH metrics beyond the general number of new hires made in the prior year. Access to detailed SAH metrics would allow you to judge whether or not your profile fits the company's culture and business needs (based on the profiles of the hired candidates). When it comes to making business decisions on where and how to sell products, companies look at detailed data that characterize their target consumers in order to optimize delivery and sales. You should adopt these same strategies in order to utilize the most effective recruitment channels used by your target companies that result in hired candidates. The more information you have on a company's SAH metrics, the better prepared you will be to optimize the delivery of your value proposition and effectively sell it.

"To assist you in your job search and decision-making process, we offer the expertise of one of our own team members. Someone who has gone through what you are now, and who knows what working at Lockheed Martin is all about. Speak directly to us in a private, virtual, real-time environment." – Lockheed Martin

1. **Judge The Differentiation Of The Recruitment Process**

Is your target employer's recruitment process just a "me too" copy of the next employer's process? It is ironic how few employers make any attempts to differentiate their recruitment processes, yet they punish job seekers who are not able to differentiate themselves from other applicants. Look for signs of selection-criteria differentiation, and customer-orientation if you go through the formal process. Assess how you are treated from the moment you visit the career site to the moment you complete the online application. When you are selected to advance through the formal process, you should take note of the total experience: the duration and rigor of the application, the timing and personalization of feedback, the relativity of the selection-criteria to the JPA, and the business acumen of the recruiters.

Most companies seem to believe in the one-size-fits-all recruitment process regardless of the myriad job applicant profiles. This only forces you to play the corporate recruitment game to your detriment. Employers who lack innovation in recruitment processes usually signal employers who have relinquished control of their talent selection to unimaginative Human Resources departments. If other business units such as Marketing, Operations, IT, and Finance are able to differentiate and customize their processes to meet constantly changing organizational goals; then it is odd that Human Resources clings to the same formal recruitment processes used by virtually every global company. If the only mechanism for recruiting talent into an organization goes through Human Resources, then that is cause for alarm and should encourage you to seek an alternative route to the Hiring Managers at your target companies.

2. **Judge The Business Acumen Of The Recruiters**

Are the recruiters more interested in filling a job posting or more interested in selecting talent for the company? The majority of recruiters screen job applicants solely on the contents of a stated JPA and are not able to see the forest for the trees. This failing of the process is detrimental to your candidacy as an employee, and it means that the wrong recruiters are in the right positions. For example, a professional sports team has Talent Scouts whose sole purpose is to look for "talent by position" and "talent by potential" when observing players who will fill future roster spots. A player may be very talented at one position but better suited to play another. This happens all the time in American football where there are countless examples of former quarterbacks now playing the wide receiver position and vice versa.

Beware the companies whose talent selection process is hijacked by incompetent recruiters who don't understand core business practices. Ideally, business-minded recruiters would write market-oriented JPA's that appeal to targeted job seekers. They would, in effect, hire the person and not the position. However, these types of recruiters are in short supply and are slowly fading into extinction. Incompetent recruiters have now taken over the talent selection "watering hole" and have crowded out their competent counterparts. If the "Masters of Talent Selection" are unable to evaluate potential talent on the front end of the SAH process, then that probably doesn't bode well for your life as an employee on the back end. Corporate recruiters who are incompetent usually foretell an incompetent Human Resources department that is disconnected from the company's core business: yet, this will be the department that sets the practices and policies that will affect every aspect of the company's EVP – go figure!

3. **Judge The Online Application & Recruitment Process**

These tell you a lot about a company's evaluation and assessment methodologies as well as how much value they place on their employer brand. If you look closely enough, you'll find that many companies include a disclaimer that states: *"Only qualified applicants will be contacted for interviews."* So how exactly should you define their meaning of qualified? There are many qualified job seekers who apply and never receive so much as a rejection email. Many recruitment processes are filled with obvious screens designed to weed out undesirable job applicants not fitting a standard mold. These processes are not the makings of a company concerned about treating each job seeker like a valued customer. However, it does speak volumes about a company's sole interest in cherry-picking the few applicants it deems are the best fit for its predefined corporate employee mold.

Recruitment processes vary from company to company but if you find that an employer has an extensive recruitment process that includes multiple interviews and assessments, then you can be assured that the company values processes over people. That is good for some job seekers and bad for others. Your challenge will be to determine when stringent recruitment processes are advantageous for you, and when they are not. How employers behave during the recruitment process is an indicator of what are accepted workplace practices. Your first clues will be found in the online application itself. The more detailed the application, the more likely it is that the company's workplace environment is drenched in bureaucracy. Online applications that require multiple tests, pre-screening questions, and written essays – to name a few – foretell of companies that value the features of their employer brand, not the actual benefits (if any).

4. **Judge The Alternative Recruitment Methods**

If companies have only one way to recruit job seekers online, then that signals a lack of creativity and an adherence to old ways of doing business. Given the technology available and the challenges companies face, every company should offer more recruitment methods than just the one-size-fits-all process driven by the applicant tracking system. Employers that lack alternative recruitment methods online are signaling that they are not interested in engaging job seekers outside of the formal processes they have designated to engage them. If you do not fit the mold for online JPA's, then these companies rarely present an alternative channel for you to make yourself known to them.

The vast majority of companies don't even offer virtual recruitment fairs, virtual recruiter chats, or virtual case competitions (crowdsourcing, business games, etc.) as a means of assessing talented job seekers. Many employers are afraid to make recruiters available to engage job seekers who have not been filtered through their online application process for fear of wasting resources on unknown people. What if one of those unknowns is the next Steve Jobs or Mark Zuckerberg? How much would the resources provided to engage those unknown people be worth then? The employers that don't maximize technology to engage the many talented job seekers in the world are either extremely shortsighted, or suffocated by shortsighted Human Resources practices – either of which doesn't bode well for their EVP.

Chapter 31
EVP Component #4: Employer Rankings Publications (ERP)

"FORTUNE's annual list, administered by the Great Place to Work Institute (GPTWI) evaluates and selects companies based on a range of criteria. The survey asks questions related to attitudes about management's credibility, job satisfaction and camaraderie, pay and benefit programs, hiring practices, internal communications, training, recognition programs and diversity efforts, among others." – www.money.cnn.com

Companies take a lot of pride in being ranked as best places to work even if they are undeserving. Many companies listed in publications that purport to judge them as best places to work or employers of choice, tend to benefit from the halo effect of their ubiquitous product brands. How else do you explain a company like Cisco being ranked as an employer of choice by various ERP's even after they announced major employee headcount reductions? **Many major companies announcing massive workforce reductions are still listed year after year in the ERP's.** It would be more balanced to include the opinions of former employees in these publications. How a company treats the employees it decides to terminate says a lot about its employer brand. Job seekers have to analyze and interpret the objective data that show a company's employee practices versus the oftentimes unknown methodology used to rank them as employers of choice. Since the rankings publications don't always provide the raw data and formulas used in the calculations, should you really trust the validity of the results? Many job seekers trust these rankings as proxies for the listed companies' EVP. A lot of factors will influence the ratings that employees give their companies; therefore, it is important to know how anonymous the surveys are and the profile of the employees taking them. Your task will be to judge these employers based on objective data you can personally validate versus what is listed on an ERP.

"Genentech Makes FORTUNE's "Best Companies to Work For" List On January 20, 2011, Genentech was included on FORTUNE's 100 "Best Companies to Work For" list for the 13th consecutive year." – Genentech

1. **Judge The Methodology Used To Rank Employers**

    You have to view ERP's with deep suspicion. Since you don't know how the rankings were compiled, who exactly was surveyed, or the breadth of questions asked; you really shouldn't put too much stock into the results. Do some research on how these ERP's actually judge employers and you'll find that these surveys function more like political polls: the results are based on a small sample population only. The rankings surveys are not given to a company's entire workforce: they are instead given to a random sample – that in reality isn't so random! If you can't trust the methodology then you can't trust the survey. These ERP's amount to little more than popularity contests for the companies that are equipped to play the rankings game. There are only three types of ERP's that get packaged and sold: 1) internal employee driven; 2) external employee driven; 3) student driven.

    With internal employees, the rankings surveys are carefully coordinated between the company and the ERP. Surely you don't think that some external rankings organization just sends an email blast to every corporate employee at global companies? How do you think they gain access to the employees who answer the surveys? Human Resources! That's right; our good friends in Human Resources facilitate this process and more often than not, decide which of the randomly selected employees will be privy to the survey. Do you think they are going to send the surveys to the average employee who has an axe to grind with the company? With external employees, the surveys hold even less weight because most of those professionals have never been employed by the companies they are ranking. To them, it's just a beauty contest of who they perceive to be the best employers. Finally, with students, the surveys are usually popularity contests based on the companies for which they dream about working. What's missing from all of these methodologies? Former employees! In my opinion, a true rankings methodology would include former employees. Be sure to carefully scrutinize the methodologies involved in the rankings before you take them at face value.

2. **Judge The Merit Of The Assigned Ranking**

If you really want to know if a company deserves its ranking as a great place to work or as an ideal employer, then you should judge that through your own research. One search on Glassdoor.com will uncover all you need to know about the veracity of an employer ranking. The employee comments, reviews, and evaluations listed on employer review sites can't always be taken as fact – but neither can the survey results from the multiple ERP's. Rankings are all based on subjective opinions. How can you consider them objective without knowing how the survey was conducted, the questions asked, or the profiles of the individuals completing the surveys? Can you really afford to blindly believe that a target employer merits its ranking based on such gaping subjectivity? To my knowledge, these same employers are not so naïve as to believe all of the subjective details of your employment application and completed interviews without conducting rigorous background checks.

Job seekers usually ignore the obvious red flags when it comes to their target companies because of a misguided affinity to be a corporate employee. This affinity conditions you to believe that an arbitrary ERP can assign a ranking that will accurately measure a company's EVP. You will be duped into believing that the companies live up to their rankings. This is a common marketing trick (EBHP) played with comparative numbers where the ERP's control which numbers will be compared, and the value given to those numbers. If you momentarily put aside the fantasy of working with your "employer of choice", you will be able to judge these companies with more clarity. How does the judgment of your ideal employer change when you read stories of their careless mismanagement of workforce reductions? How does it change when you read of their involvement in questionable labor practices outside of your home country? How does it change when you read of their contribution to environmental degradation? Of course, these and many more questions will depend upon your personal ethics, values, and convictions. As long as you take into consideration how your target employers actually behave versus how some third-party ERP ranks them, then that will allow you to judge the merit of the assigned ranking.

Chapter 32
EVP Component #5: Employee Engagement Report (EER)

"Employee engagement is absolutely essential for building retention and improved performance within a business organization. Research has it that employees who are committed to their work perform better." - www.employeeengagementsurvey.net

It is important that you know whether a company has a functional or dysfunctional workplace. Knowing a company's employee engagement report scores is absolutely critical to judging a company's EVP. This will allow you to determine the relative satisfaction of your potential co-workers and any other major issues that you might want to investigate. The surveys that measure employee engagement go by many names: Organizational Health Surveys, Global People Surveys, and Voice of the Employee. It is understandable that a company with a low overall engagement score will not want to publish this information on its website. However, this is the very reason why new employees feel misled after experiencing a less than stellar workplace environment: which could lead to early disengagement and loss of productivity. **The majority of companies do not publish any metrics from their EER's while some only publish the overall percentage of their workforce that completed the survey.** It's not enough for companies to only publish a few EER metrics: they should publish the results of the key questions and scores that would most affect your decision to apply - or accept an employment offer.

"Our employee engagement metric is based on comprehensive employee surveys that measure a combination of commitment, pride, loyalty, and personal advocacy for SAP. In 2010, 49% of a representative, random sample of employees at all levels - above the industry benchmark - took part in our pulse check survey." - SAP

1. **Judge The Red Flags For Employees**

If you're lucky, you'll find an employer who has listed at least a few of the questions asked on their most recent EER – but only if you're lucky! It just doesn't happen often; and when it does, the questions are handpicked by the company. The only way you can accurately judge employee engagement is to see all of the questions that were asked – along with the results – and then benchmark them against similar companies. The problem is that none of the other companies make their results available; so for lack of transparency, you're back to square one. Many companies that publish their EER results will oftentimes obscure the lowest numbers, or use employer branding hocus pocus to marginalize their impact.

There are always tell-tell signs of employee discontent and you need to gauge the EER results carefully to look for trends that go in the wrong direction. This information will help you determine what is prioritized by management as it concerns employee engagement. It is important to know whether or not management is doing anything to improve the situation, or if they are just turning a blind eye. Many companies use EER surveys like politicians use polls: they just want to concentrate on the hot-button issues to placate the masses. However, this may not be sufficient for your unique concerns. There is no perfect workplace environment. Don't pursue employment at your target companies without understanding the sentiments of the very people whose disposition will make your employment a heaven or hell. Pay attention to EER statistics that could be canaries in the coal mine because they will warrant further investigation.

2. **Judge The White Flags For Management**

The EER can be a goldmine of information for how well an employer listens to its employees. If you see positive trends in the EER scores then that is a good sign. When analyzing EER's, be sure to look at the survey results for the prior three years at a minimum. In the case where the company only does the survey every 2 years, you'll need to look at the prior three survey results if possible. Why? Because you want to look for evidence that management has, in effect, waved the white flag on the issues that are red flags for employees. There may be some issues within an organization that management has just decided it will live with.

This is no different than a company deciding to live with high turnover for its jobs that are low-paid or dead-ends. It's just a cost of doing business that many companies are unwilling (or unable) to improve without committing serious financial resources (which they are loath to do). Your objective needs to be to determine how your target companies deal with employee engagement issues that are important to you. There is no exact science in determining these white flags: so don't look for some silver-bullet formula or metric to give you an answer. You will have to base your judgments on the data that is available and what you feel should be acceptable. For example, what does it say about a company's management team and priorities if the number of employees stating, *"I have the resources to perform my job well"*, declines or remains at a low rate for 3 years in a row? That is the level of critical thinking you will need to use in your analysis of the EER's.

Chapter 33
EVP Component #6: Work-Life Benefits (WLB)

"Many of our employees take advantage of work-life options offered by HP. In our annual Voice of the Workforce survey, our work-life programs have been consistently identified as very popular among employees." – Hewlett-Packard

If you value benefits such as telecommuting, flexible schedules, and paid time off; then you definitely need to judge the likelihood that you'll be able to enjoy those benefits – and more – before applying to a JPA. **It's not enough to know that the company merely offers these benefits, but that it actually embraces them.** WLB's are very important to all employees regardless of their age. It entails creating practices that facilitate flexibility in working hours to incorporating the life changes of an employee in ways that maximize productivity. Many companies state that they observe WLB concerns, but offer no objective data to support those claims. It will be a rarity if you find any meaningful metrics characterizing a company's WLB's. Unfortunately for you, it won't be easy to judge if a workplace culture frowns upon (or covertly punishes) employees who request a flexible schedule, sabbatical, leave of absence, or time off to care for a dependent. Companies that invest in WLB's and have strategies to manage their effects on business outcomes will be the winners in the bid to attract and retain high-performance workers. To be more transparent, companies should publish more than just broad and appealing statements about WLB's: but of course, that would make it too easy for you. Therefore, it is important to judge whether or not a company can provide metrics that prove its WLB's are encouraged and supported by the workplace environment.

"Managing your career and your personal life can be challenging. Intel is committed to making it easier. We want to help our employees make the most of both worlds. Whether you are a parent or have education goals, eldercare responsibilities, or just some of life's details to attend to, we have a variety of programs in place around the world to help." – Intel

1. **Judge The Probability Of WLB Usage**

It's nice that some employers loudly promote their WLB's on every corner of their CSC's and other promotional publications they use to entice potential employees to apply (or accept a job) to a JPA. However, all those benefits don't mean a thing if you don't have unfettered access to use them. What companies forget to tell you – on purpose, I might add – is that some of these benefits come with strings attached: such as wait periods and supervisor approvals. Just because an employer promotes a lot of cool WLB's on their websites and marketing materials doesn't necessarily mean that you'll be able to enjoy them when you want to. Take for example, the sabbatical. This was once the chief domain of academics until companies realized that non-academics could benefit from a paid (or unpaid) absence from their jobs to pursue a personal (or professional) activity.

For many companies, seven years is the average time you will need to be employed before you are granted the opportunity to request a sabbatical. That's right, seven entire years in a world where the average new hire is probably not going to remain with the same employer for more than 2 years. Even if you wanted to stay with an employer for the long term, the decision really is out of your hands given the probability that the company can restructure, get acquired, or go out of business altogether before you reach that dear seven-year mark. Furthermore, your request is subject to approval by your supervisor and his Human Resources counterpart. Another example is the option to work a flexible schedule. Again, while this may seem like a benefit open to every employee, it will largely depend on your supervisor's needs and whether or not he believes it is justified. Do not be swindled into believing that upon becoming an employee, you will be granted free access to use WLB's as you choose.

2. **Judge The Support For WLB Usage**

The larger question that job seekers need to answer pertaining to WLB's is whether or not the company is committed to employee sustainability or if they are just into employee "burn and churn". You will be hard-pressed to find corporate employees who only work the standard work-week hours as defined by their employers. Technology facilitates an extended work-week beyond the office cubicle, and it has almost become the *de facto* standard that you will work well beyond normal business hours. This can lead to employee burnout if not carefully managed. Given today's job pressures with more work being done by fewer people, it's a recipe for disaster. Every corporate job comes with its fair share of unpaid overtime work and that is part of the deal you make when you become a corporate employee.

The problem is when unpaid overtime becomes part of the norm and you are expected to work 60-plus hours per week just to meet ever-tightening deadlines along with increased workloads. If the workplace environment is that busy and that demanding, do you really think your employer is going to approve of your working a flexible schedule? Do you really think you'll be looked upon as a "dedicated employee" if you request a short-term leave of absence or sabbatical? If the company does not embrace the very policies and practices it has in place to ensure the mental and physical sustainability of its employees, then that is cause for alarm. If you thrive in a demanding workplace environment that requires 60-plus hours a week of your time, then it's not a problem. But if you have other commitments or activities you would like to integrate into your working life, then you will want to carefully judge this aspect of a company's EVP.

Chapter 34
EVP Component #7: Volunteering And Sustainability Investments (VSI)

"Barclays employees around the world are encouraged to give their time, energy and skills to the causes they care about, supported with paid time away from work and team grants." – Barclays

How a company values and supports employee volunteers can communicate a lot about its people practices. Social responsibility is not just confined to a company's financial support of social organizations and programs, but also to its support of employees' social activities and involvement. Look for evidence of the company's active promotion of these activities to its employees. **Corporate Social Responsibility is no longer just for investors and government regulators to judge, but also for job seekers and employees.** Companies have seized on this phenomenon to not only attract and retain high performing workers, but also to build their brands and businesses in the communities in which they operate. What started out as philanthropy from the corporate coffers has transformed into a powerful force for social change and development. While companies tout on their websites all the organizations they support and how many volunteer hours per year they contribute to various causes; what doesn't get clearly communicated is how employee volunteer activities are valued, promoted, and supported by the company. It is also not always clear how a company's social investments are aligned with its business or values. The companies that make social investments purely for tax purposes – or for compliance reasons – are usually the ones that will make it difficult for you to actively participate in VSI activities.

"Our Employees regularly volunteer their time and donate to the causes that are closest to their hearts. In 2010, Southwest Airlines Employees volunteered more than 80,000 hours to charities across the country, donated to other Southwest Airlines Employees in need, and had a direct

impact on charitable organizations within their community." – Southwest

1. **Judge The Value To Employees' Career Growth**

It's all too easy to think that volunteering activities will have no impact on your career, but that is an old school way of thinking. Today's employers place a premium on job seekers who display skills and values gained through volunteer work because it allows them to judge their work ethic and passion. But just how these skills are valued is up for debate, and something you need to have clear before becoming an employee. For example, what is the career path for employees who volunteer for company-sponsored organizations? You should look for any trends or evidence showing that VSI's supported by the company are also officially recognized by the company. Do companies include volunteer activities in employees' formal performance evaluations? Verbal recognition and wood-stained plaques are flattering, but they are easily forgotten if they are not recorded in your personnel file. Employers that identify the career development and skills gained from volunteer activities that improve employees' work performance use VSI's as a competitive advantage. Do you know the percentage of employees who actively volunteer at your target companies? If not, you should make it a point to find out and look for trends that show participation rates moving in one direction or the other.

Employees themselves are the best gauge as to whether or not volunteer activities are useful to their career advancement and opportunities: pay special attention to any objective metrics that answer your questions in those areas. A company's community involvement philosophy, as well as career development philosophy, will determine how it assesses employee involvement in its VSI's. Do not assume that companies will properly assess the competencies you develop through volunteering: even if the company supports your activities. The irony is that today's business leaders are increasingly becoming board members of non-profit organizations in order to develop their own ksa's in addition to providing these non-profits with much needed business expertise. Given that fact, it would be a shame if these same employers did not fully support and promote the value that volunteering will have on the careers of its employees. Beware the companies that do not have systems in place to encourage volunteering as a means to support its social investments, and also to provide professional development opportunities to its employees.

2. **Judge The Value To A Company's Business Growth**

Are social investments viewed by the company as a core value aligned with their business, or as a cost of being a corporate citizen? For example, if the majority of activities sponsored by a company have no clear business alignment, then what does that say for the value of those activities to the company's growth? What you should be looking for are the employers who practice sustainability and environmental stewardship because it is essential to growing their financial capital as well as social and human capital. If you feel strongly about a company's involvement in activities, programs, and events that affect quality of life and the environment; then it is essential to verify the company's commitment before considering them a target employer. Beware the companies that don't provide transparent performance assessments of the activities they support. They are either hiding poor numbers, or don't have any value for assessing their VSI activities.

It is not about how much money a company commits each year to social investments; it is more about how they leverage those investments to improve their business outcomes. For example, a company in the pharmaceutical industry partnering with health-oriented non-profit organizations would be able to leverage that relationship to better serve its markets. Engagement with these organizations expands a company's business by helping to improve product design, effectiveness, and delivery. That in turn increases the scale and scope of potential consumers to grow the business. When a company values its social investments as integral to its business strategy, then you can rest assured that there will be a deep commitment. If it is beneficial for the company, then it will be beneficial for your career if you volunteer to support those partnerships. Pay special attention to the number of leaders at your target companies who are board members for non-profit organizations: what bodes well for the top leaders usually bodes well for everyone else in the company.

Chapter 35
EVP Component #8: Career Mobility And Development (CMD)

"Internal mobility is a growth factor as it provides the opportunity to learn firsthand about the different businesses and to take on different competencies throughout a professional career." – Repsol

With changes in the flow of capital investments and business interests, it's important to judge how companies prepare their employees to take on professional challenges. Statements about a company's cumulative training hours for its workforce are meaningless. You should be looking for clues to determine the company's track record for investing in its people. CMD is an important factor that you must take into consideration when evaluating potential employers. Mobility has taken on a broader definition in the global economy and now includes geographic mobility in addition to inter and intra-company mobility. Some companies even have programs that allow employees to do short-term assignments with selected suppliers or service providers. Development includes both formal training and performance management discussions: **both are essential to a company's continued competitiveness and ability to maintain an employable workforce.** There isn't much to judge when companies only publish general numbers for employee training hours per year, employees working internationally, and employees receiving formal performance management discussions. Unless these metrics are specific, transparent, and detailed; they do little to prove that a company values CMD.

"We invest in our people and have developed a series of special programs that facilitate young team members as they pursue a career that fulfills their ambitions and potential." – Dell

1. **Judge The Career Management Philosophy Of The Company**

    It is no longer a company's responsibility to be the caretaker of your career: those days are long gone and will not return. Even though employers offer training and development opportunities for their employees, it is still up to the individual employee to take advantage of them. Job seekers need to ascertain as much as possible whether or not an employer focuses solely on the development of selected high-potential employees. Why? Because if you are not deemed to be a "corporate promotable", all those CMD opportunities sold to you during the recruitment process won't mean anything. Discovering the CMD philosophy of a company allows you to make a realistic assessment of what you can expect as an employee. If you are not interviewing for – or hired into – an employer's leadership program for high-potential employees, then you need to have a clear strategy (and timeline) to obtain your career objectives (without the assistance of the corporate leadership team).

It is all too easy for job seekers to believe they will have access to the entire menu of an employer's CMD's because of what they see and hear on the CSC's. During the recruitment process you will be told that plenty of professional opportunities await you "if" you perform well. What isn't listed on the CSC's or discussed with you during interviews are the actual metrics that show the performance ratings and assessments of the employees who actually do enjoy the full benefits of CMD's. Some companies have CMD philosophies based on workplace meritocracies that allow anyone displaying certain leadership and performance characteristics to advance. That sounds very good and plausible if there is transparency in how a company measures and determines those characteristics. Other companies might have a more egalitarian CMD where star performers and average performers are treated like one and the same. Good for you if you're an average worker, but bad if you consider yourself a star performer. It's to your advantage to know the intricate details of a company's CMD policies and practices before becoming an employee.

2. **Judge The Effectiveness Of Employee Development Practices**

It's not about the quantity of training courses and development opportunities offered by an employer; it's more about the quality and impact they have on your career and the organization. You won't find any measures of CMD effectiveness on the company's website; therefore, you will have to find alternative means to gather useable metrics to answer your concerns. For example, what information can you glean from an employer only listing the total number of training hours per year provided to its employees? Just knowing the average number of hours provided per year tells you nothing of how the company benefited from the investment. Companies that do not have reliable means (or no means at all) for measuring the business impact of their CMD's will usually reduce investment in those areas or justify not providing opportunities. In rare cases, you might find listed on a company's career site the number (or percentage) of its employees working abroad. That's all good and great, but it would be nice to know the percentage of managers and other company leaders who also worked internationally. This will at least give you an idea of how crucial these assignments are to your future career development and the employer's business objectives.

You don't want to fall prey to the *"out of sight, out of mind"* phenomenon that can sometimes befall globetrotting employees. It's crucial to understand how a company measures the effectiveness of its performance management system because it will be used by HR and Hiring Managers to rate and evaluate you regarding your career development and advancement. Poorly-designed CMD's are worse than having none at all. Look for companies that have a high completion rate of annual performance evaluations in addition to a high frequency rate of evaluations given per employee in a calendar year. Given the speed at which business strategies change in relation to the marketplace, it is no longer sensible (nor effective) to have once-a-year performance evaluations. Most companies do not make performance management data available to prying eyes. However, you will need to investigate whether or not the performance management processes used by your target companies are a sham (or scam, if you prefer). Otherwise, you may find yourself working hard and smart, but without receiving any measurable recognition (financial and non-financial) from your manager.

Chapter 36
EVP Component #9: Diversity And Inclusion (DAI)

"Diversity is at the very core of our ability to serve our clients well and to maximize return for our shareholders. Diversity supports and strengthens the firm's culture, and it reinforces our reputation as the employer of choice in our industry and beyond." – Goldman Sachs

In a multicultural and global marketplace, you should judge the makeup of a company's workplace across broad diversity measures like age groups, genders, ethnicities, nationalities, sexual orientation, education, experiences, ideas, personalities, lifestyles, and other unique attributes. This will give you insights into the company's progressiveness in attracting and integrating talent. DAI practices have greatly changed in form and function since they first became part of the corporate lexicon. A company's ability to integrate its employees' unique attributes can significantly impact its bottom line as well as employer brand. The vast majority of global companies have DAI programs; however, they fail to give any meaningful metrics that would be useful to prospective job seekers. Most limit their published DAI metrics to the number of women and disabled employees hired, which while good for public relations, doesn't provide details on their impact to the company. **What does not get communicated in a measurable way is how a company's complete definition of a diverse workforce is distributed and utilized throughout the workplace.** If you desire a workplace that allows you to interact with diverse people in an environment where you can maximize your own unique attributes, then it is essential to look beyond the average company-provided metrics.

"At ABB, diversity means difference –differences that make each of us unique. This includes tangible differences such as age, gender, ethnicity, physical disability and appearance as well as underlying differences such as beliefs, ways of thinking and acting. Inclusion means understanding, valuing and respecting workplace diversity, so that no employee is

excluded from the workplace nor the opportunity to develop skills and talents consistent with our values and business objectives." – ABB

1. **Judge The Business Impact On The Company**

In today's globally-connected world, it is unfortunate that DAI is not always leveraged as the strategic advantage that it is. There are too many companies focused solely on hiring different workers to meet their diversity goals, but they lack any strategy for how that diversity should be embraced and utilized to impact the business. There is still a lack of workplace policies and practices to create an inclusive environment for all workers to use their full capabilities to the benefit of their colleagues and the company. What mechanisms does the company have in place to allow you to find talented individuals within the workforce who can assist you with your job? How do companies measure the impact of its employees who contribute to the professional success of colleagues working on different teams and in different business units? Beware the companies that don't have a means to measure how their DAI gives them a competitive advantage in the global market. The companies that underutilize and overlook the unique ksa's possessed by their own workforce do so at the expense of their business performance and sustainability.

Many employers fail miserably to build inclusive workplace environments that encourage employees to utilize their non-work related ksa's. This is a fatal flaw in the way these companies define ksa's and doesn't take advantage of the ksa's you don't use on the job, or those that you use outside of the job. Look for the employers who have a firm strategy for integrating your best skills into its workplace and business strategy. Beware the companies who only look to recruit across DAI metrics in order to comply with legal mandates. DAI has been expanded to include more measures besides the visible characteristics of an employee. You should have your own definition for what you consider to be appropriate DAI. Therefore, look for companies that provide broad measures and statistics that allow you to understand their DAI philosophy and how it is integrated into their business strategy. Think about why companies like Apple,

Google, and Virgin Atlantic are successful. Look at their leadership and workforce to determine just how their DAI breakdown is a contributing factor. Employers that can leverage their DAI to improve their workplace engagement are better positioned to achieve improvements for the products (and services) provided to their customers and clients.

2. **Judge The Perception Of Employees And Management**

More important than anything regarding an employer's DAI practices and policies is how the employees and managers themselves perceive its impact on the company. Again, this is information that won't be found on a company's website and may not be something the company even measures. If indeed it is not measured, then that too, speaks volumes about its perception. As a job seeker, the last thing you want to do is to work for a company that has not clearly communicated its DAI activities, let alone one that has not educated its workforce on what DAI means to the company and why every employee falls under the broad spectrum of DAI. What usually happens is that DAI becomes branded as a company's attempt to hire and integrate the *"others"* into the fabric of the workplace. This can sometimes sow the seeds of misunderstanding, resistance, and contempt for the so-called *"others"*. Beware of companies that have unwittingly sabotaged their own DAI efforts because of a failure to provide proper communication and training to their workforce. Many of these companies don't fully utilize DAI as a strategy to unleash the creativity, engagement, and passion of their employees to deliver sustainable stakeholder value.

Most large companies are still stuck in the old "seniority rules" model: meaning that young employees will rarely have a major voice within the company – let alone the confidence of the senior leaders who make the business decisions. If companies are willing to eschew DAI strategies to continue the "seniority rules" model, then imagine what that means for all the other employee characteristics and qualities that are not based on years of service (or years of experience). Look for evidence that a company is grounded in the belief that ideas, innovation, motivation, and leadership can come from any employee in the corporate hierarchy and geography. Certify as much as possible that a company includes every single employee in its DAI strategies as opposed to only focusing on the employees who fall outside the "norm" of the company's employee profile. DAI strategies are oftentimes designed and implemented in ways that exempt employees representing the "majority group" (based on nationality, race, religion, gender, age, education, etc.) from being included. Judge employers on how they use DAI as a shared business strategy to create a healthy workplace environment, purposeful collaborations, and optimal engagement.

Chapter 37
EVP Component #10: Web 2.0 Technologies (W2T)

"Cisco is using Web 2.0 technologies to enable collaboration between employees, partners, and customers, yielding increased productivity and deeper relationships. Leveraging other Web 2.0 technologies, such as blogs and wikis, and new business models, such as social networking and folksonomies, the company is increasing peer-to-peer collaboration and ideation and transforming key business processes." – Cisco

In the social media age, it is paramount to judge a company's use of W2T's on their employee intranets. A company that makes use of these technologies to connect its entire workforce will facilitate more effective collaboration and overall performance. **You do not want to waste your time applying to a company that is intent on blocking W2T collaboration in its workplace.** With the ubiquity of social media, companies need to find ways to integrate the power of these collaborative technologies into their workplace practices. In the beginning of the social media boom, most companies sought to block these technologies on their intranets for fear of diminished employee productivity. Time has proven that to be a huge mistake. Nowadays, many companies have embraced these technologies and have upgraded their own internal intranets to include social media-styled collaboration between their employees. A lot of companies publicize that they have collaborative workplace environments, but very few actually encourage the use of collaborative technologies that are accessible by their entire workforce. If a company's intranet has not been upgraded with W2T, then that signals a lack of value for using technology to optimize professional collaboration. If you value online social networking as a tool for learning, sharing, and business development; then you will want to work for an employer that does the same.

"NI Talk has been extremely successful. In 2010, NI sought to help employees collaborate more efficiently across teams worldwide. In the first nine months of use, NI Talk had more than 3,200 users, more than

1,700 groups, 15,589 documents, and 7,119 discussions generating more than 26,000 responses." – National Instruments

1. **Judge The Use Of External Social Media Tools**

The vast majority of employers have yet to use social media to engage job seekers on a personal level. Some companies don't even use them while others only make use of them to communicate news about their products and services. Worse still, the companies that do use distinct social media tools on their CSC's only provide a one-way street of communication at best. While these companies might like to think that pushing out random news related to jobs and careers is engaging job seekers, it is actually no different than professional spamming. Job seekers are not looking for more random, subjective information that will not add any value to their job search goals. The whole point of social media is to be social and to allow for a real-time exchange of communication with an actual person.

Most corporate recruiters at global companies will not engage job seekers in two-way conversations via social media. They haven't fully embraced social media as a transformative recruitment tool and are instead clinging to the old ways of doing business: you apply, they select. What conclusions should you draw if you value collaborative W2T's, yet the company does not even effectively use them to engage you as a job seeker? It is difficult to imagine that such a company would fully embrace the use of W2T's in the workplace. Nevertheless, many global companies do leverage W2T's in their customer service departments as well as marketing departments. Companies such as the Four Seasons Hotels and Zappos strategically use social media tools to engage their customers and clients who purchase their products and services. I guess you, as a job seeker, are just not that important to warrant W2T engagement.

2. **Judge The Company's Social Media Integration**

Working for a company that is behind the technological curve and not showing signs of catching up is probably not in your best interest. These types of companies are wedded to outdated business practices. They don't exhibit the ability (or desire) to adapt technology as a competitive advantage as it pertains to their people practices. Given the fact that the vast majority of W2T's are freely available for everyone's use, there is no excuse for a company not to have them integrated on its intranets. At the very least, companies can create their own internal knock-offs. Very few of the companies that are listed as best places to work provide any detail of the type of W2T's they use (if any). This is something that you will want to know in advance of applying to (or accepting) a job because it will have huge implications on your job performance as well as the company's performance. Even if you don't use W2T's much in your personal life, the benefits of working for a company that allows employees to use them far outweigh your W2T shortcomings. Why? Because they allow others in the workplace to easily locate and leverage each other's talents for the company's benefit.

Companies that are quick to adapt W2T's that are low cost (and in most cases no cost!) can gain significant advantages over their competitors in myriad internal and external business metrics. For example, if you are evaluating five companies, and four of those companies encourage open use of social media within the workplace to facilitate project collaboration; then what will you think of the one company that doesn't offer that opportunity? Think of how the music and print industries (among others) were slow to adapt to the disruptive changes of the internet. They chose to fight the technological advances instead of embracing them and adapting new business models to leverage them: that story didn't end well for them. You need to develop questions that will give you a clear indication of a company's policies, practices, and strategies regarding W2T's. You also need to look for objective indications of how its current employees use them. If you find that some of your target employers are lacking in W2T's, it does not mean you have to automatically exclude the company from employment consideration: it may well be an opportunity for you to pitch the value proposition for why the company should integrate W2T's – with you as the project manager.

3. **Judge The Business Impact Of Social Media**

It is all too easy to think that companies are all-seeing and all-knowing as it regards the business impacts made by rapidly advancing W2T's: but this is not true. You should make it your job to identify the positive and negative impacts that specific technologies can have on your target companies. Doing this will put you head and shoulders above your job seeking competitors. It also allows you to identify how a company is currently using (or not using) W2T's to engage its internal and external customers. Would your target companies benefit from W2T's in ways that would improve their business metrics? How are they currently using W2T's to improve product design, employee collaboration, and customer service? It will be a rare occasion if you find the answers to any of these questions on a company's CSC's. You'll have to do in-depth networking and informational interviewing to assess the business usage of a target company's W2T's. Otherwise, you might find yourself trying to work for a company that can be made obsolete by current W2T's, or that is being severely disrupted by them.

There are a lot of factors to consider when investigating the business impact of a company's W2T's. How a company benefits will depend on its leadership, flexibility, and adaptability regarding technological advances. Job seekers often fail to realize that it is their responsibility to think like a business: no longer can you merely "outsource" that responsibility to a company. How disruptive is "cloud computing" (offered by Google and Amazon) on the companies whose entire business is built on selling fixed and portable memory drives? You need only think of how quickly radio, television, and print advertising dollars dried up since the growth of W2T's. Now companies can more precisely spend their advertising dollars to reach the potential buyers of their products. This is the level of depth you need to delve into when evaluating the myriad impacts W2T's have on global businesses. If the recruiters and Hiring Managers you speak with at your target companies seem oblivious to how their companies are leveraging W2T's, then that means any or both of the following: 1) they have a low regard for internet and social media technologies; 2) they don't understand the business value of them.

Chapter 38
EVP Component #11: Recognition And Compensation (RAC)

"You will find that we offer a range of recognition programs and awards that acknowledge individuals and teams for their outstanding achievements and service. These acknowledgements may take the form of cash awards or special recognition." – Lockheed Martin

Intrinsic rewards can be just as valuable as extrinsic ones in the workplace. If you expect to work with a company that recognizes your achievements with more than just a bonus check or salary increase, then you'll be looking for the ones that value peer recognition as well. **A pat on the back is good now and then, but formal recognition for a job well-done is the hallmark of a great workplace environment.** Many companies realize the benefits of recognizing employees who perform exceptional work, and duly publish their RAC programs on their CSC's. Most only publish general statements saying they recognize high achievers, or list the names of specific rewards offered. Having formal RAC programs can motivate employees to perform at a high level and nurture a performance-based culture. If you are a job seeker who is accustomed to competing for individual and team accolades, then you will want to work with companies that recognize achievements in creative ways. Beware the companies that only pay lip service to RAC programs. They will expect you to exceed expectations on every project, work as many hours as it takes to get the job done, and put the company's interests ahead of your personal interests; however, you will rarely receive any RAC worth bragging about. Job seekers who desire to be recognized for their above-average contributions in the workplace need to know the depth of a company's RAC policies and practices. Most global companies only show a list of RAC programs on offer, but with no current (or transparent) metrics to support them.

"As your career progresses, your income increases. At Siemens we have very competitive base salaries in all countries. However, we believe that special dedication and achievement warrant special recognition, which is

why we offer a performance-related bonus system as well as a share-matching program." – Siemens

1. **Judge Whether Employees Are Treated As Costs Or Assets**

    There are companies that view employees as a "cost of doing business", and others that view them as an "asset for growing business". This distinction is important, and you will need to know to which philosophy your target employers subscribe. Companies that treat employees as costs are the ones that are constantly slashing employee headcount in reaction to poor earnings and slow growth. They pay miserable salaries, and don't have any concept of rewarding high-performance employees either financially or non-financially. Look for evidence that a company treats its people as valuable resources that are assets and essential to the company's future. These are the companies that will reward performance, offer top salaries, and invest in your development. For example, how would you judge a company that underpays and overworks its employees? How would you judge a company that pays every employee the same regardless of performance? It's safe to say that you wouldn't want to work for a company like that. While the executives and shareholders are handsomely rewarded for their work, the average corporate employee will be shamelessly shortchanged for his.

    By analyzing objective metrics characterizing a company's RAC programs, you can more easily recognize its philosophy on treating employees as costs versus assets. Beware the companies that seem overly preoccupied with your salary history before even speaking with you! Those are the companies that are more concerned about price rather than quality. It's safe to say that if they are trying to lowball you on the front end, then they will lowball you on the backend through scant salary raises, low-quality training, and skimpy profit sharing. Avoid playing the "Salary In A Box" game! You cannot fit yourself into someone else's predetermined value for a given job that doesn't take into consideration your unique ksa's. The best companies to work for will be the ones that are upfront about the value they have placed on a specific JPA so that you don't have to play guessing games. Companies that publish transparent RAC's on their JPA's and CSC's give you an opportunity to objectively judge their view of employees.

2. Judge Whether Employees Are Rewarded By Seniority Versus Performance

There is no perfect RAC scheme that will satisfy every job seeker because each individual's expectations are as different as the companies for which they desire to work. If your only focus is salary, then decisions you make about employment will be based on that one dimension – which is very limiting given the scope of other compensation factors. A wiser path to take is to look for evidence that your target employers align pay with performance. That will broaden the range of opportunities and lead to a more sustainable career. The problem in many companies is that their compensation schemes are tied to antiquated practices that merely reward "service time" – better stated as, "time in place". These practices no longer function in today's workplaces where innovation and strategic initiatives can come from anyone, regardless of age and professional experience level. Look for companies that have clear policies and practices regarding performance pay, and look for objective evidence that supports them.

Smart companies will have creative ways to fairly compensate high-performers regardless of age, employee level, or seniority. It would be a shame for you to get hired by a company only to find that if you exceed expectations, it will be met with little more than a pat on the back. The companies that are well-organized in managing their employees as assets will communicate clear expectations on how high-performance is rewarded and the impact it has on career advancement. Does the company assign top projects to staff based on seniority or based on performance? If it is the former, you might find yourself working below your potential. You don't reap the benefits of a RAC program by working below your potential! Many employers are proud to promote their supposed performance-based cultures through their CSC's. However, self-aggrandizing statements extolling the virtues of their performance management systems are largely over-rated. Without deeper inspection and supporting metrics, you will not know the value of a company's performance-based culture, or how that company nurtures and promotes it. Be sure that your expectations of RAC programs are aligned with the policies and practices of your target companies. Otherwise, companies will be merely talking loud and saying nothing, but you'll be the one working hard and getting paid nothing!

Chapter 39
EVP Component #12: Workforce Sustainability Policies (WSP)

"Lockheed Martin Corporation announced in June that of the 28,000 employees in its Aeronautics business unit it was shedding about 1,500 workers to improve affordability and to increase operational efficiency. Many workers are being offered voluntary buyout packages." - www.huffingtonpost.com

There is no such thing as a lifelong employment contract: any job seeker planning to have a long career with only one company will find it difficult to achieve. Even if you could have a lifelong employment contract, would you want it? That would assume your career goals and the company's business needs will always be in lock-step – which is entirely unrealistic. What job seekers should focus on is a company's philosophy for managing the retention and transition of its workforce as it pertains to creating a sustainable, productive, and stable workplace environment. **It's very important to discover how companies will manage the employability of their workforce during times of mass layoffs, weak profits, and spin-offs – among other unforeseen events.** In today's competitive market, there is a heightened risk of unexpected unemployment, reduced compensation, and limited career mobility. Therefore, it is essential to know a company's policy towards mitigating these risks to your livelihood. WSP's are not job security, but rather, peace of mind that comes with knowing your target employers have strategies in place to protect the interests of their workforce – just as they do to protect the interests of their shareholders. WSP's are what a company has in place to mitigate the effects of adverse market conditions (and adverse decisions made by company leaders) on employment status, compensation, benefits, and job roles.

"Drugmaker Merck has told employees it can't reach its goal of cutting up to 13,000 jobs by 2015 just by eliminating vacant jobs, so it is speeding up layoffs in the U.S." - www.nj.com

1. **Judge The Company's Record On Voluntary Turnover**

Many companies do not list any useable statistics regarding the number of employees who voluntarily leave. The voluntary turnover percentage is more important than many job seekers realize because it is a good predictor of the value of a company's workplace environment. You may have to regard any statistics you are given by a company as watered down at best. When employees leave jobs at major companies, the Human Resources department usually conducts exit interviews with them. Depending on the method used to collect the exit interview data, the employees may or may not detail the true reasons behind their departure. In spite of that limitation, you should attempt to gather metrics on the profiles of the employees who are leaving because that could indicate unresolved workplace issues. For example, if you discover that employees at certain career levels are exiting the company in droves, then that could signal CMD problems. Other things to look for would be the timing of employee departures: analyze them for trends coinciding with any major events in the company's operations, or the marketplace (mergers, offshoring, spin-offs, downsizings, recessions, etc.). This information can give you insights into the company's employee retention strategies. It would be a serious problem if a company is unable to retain its high-performing employees during times of change: especially given the fact that change is the norm.

In reality, it is usually the high-performing workers who voluntarily leave a company because they can more readily find new employment. They have ksa's that are demanded in the job market and are coveted by many companies. Look for employers that have mechanisms in place to select and engage the employees who drive business results. Otherwise, you might find yourself heading for the exits too if you choose the wrong employer. Knowing a company's employee retention strategies will also inform you about which employee profiles companies are keen to retain, and how the company goes about determining who those employees are. There will be myriad reasons why people voluntarily leave their employers, and not all of them are due to a negative reason. But having an idea of why employees leave, and the types of employees who leave is important to your judgment process. *"Why are you looking for a job?"* That is one of the main questions (after the salary question, of course) a recruiter or Hiring Manager will ask you regardless of the job search method you choose. In the case that you're an employed job seeker, the question is an attempt to know why you want to leave your current employer. If it is important for a company to know your reasons for wanting to voluntarily leave a company to join theirs, then it should be just as important for you to find out why past employees have voluntarily left theirs.

2. **Judge The Company's Record On Involuntary Turnover**

A company's ability to manage its employee headcount can make the difference between its success and its failure. What should concern you is the way that it carries out the task. It is understandable that a company may have to make slight changes to its headcount during adverse business conditions. But it is an entirely different story if employees are the ones bearing the brunt of the fiscal and strategic missteps caused by the company's leadership. The lines can become blurred when companies claim to make mass layoffs in the name of business sustainability – the *de facto* excuse. These same companies do not usually turn to their employees as a source of innovation and competitive advantage during times of financial crisis. They rely on short-term fixes like furloughs, early retirements, and mass layoffs. The more important question is how these companies treat the employees who have been loyal to them. Are these employees provided with any extended benefits such as career counseling, job retraining, and severance packages to help them transition between jobs? Does the company even track the job placement of employees who are terminated? Answers to these questions will tell you about a company's philosophy for managing the transition of its employees affected by circumstances beyond their control.

Beware the companies that use layoffs, furloughs, and reductions in compensation and benefits as business strategies to compete in the marketplace. Those are companies that lack imagination and more than likely have a leadership team that is "managing up" (concerned about major shareholders) as opposed to "managing down" (concerned about leveraging employee brain power). Look for companies that have a competent strategy for managing its workforce transitions through the ups and downs of market demand and unforeseen competitive forces. This will give you a sense of the likelihood of being affected by unexpected unemployment, or having your compensation temporarily (or permanently) reduced. No company will ever voluntarily provide you with any details of policies and practices that are unpopular with its employees. However, when you become a corporate employee, you will base your standard of living on the compensation you are paid. How would you react if you were suddenly informed that your pay and benefits will be reduced by 20% until business conditions improve? Would you be prepared for such a scenario without putting an undue burden on yourself and those who depend on you? It is in your best interest to inquire about a company's WSP's so that you can evaluate their adequacy for your employment sustainability. The sooner you know where the company's WSP deficiencies are, the sooner you can devise the proper risk management strategies to compensate.

Chapter 40
Summary: Assessing The Employer Value Proposition

"We expect our new hires to meet highly demanding standards, in terms of both background and qualifications. But we also offer extensive career opportunities, in more than 500 professional disciplines." – Total

Lack of transparency for key EVP metrics can severely affect the decisions you make in your job search. The majority of companies fail to provide detailed and explanatory metrics. However, do not mistake this failure as a mere oversight by your target companies. This is all part of the corporate recruitment game. Human Resources departments sell EVP to job seekers and current employees under the guise of employer branding (EB) campaigns. However, the manner in which EVP is assessed and sold to the public is not completely transparent, and will leave you with far more questions than answers. In order to have your questions answered, you are obliged to apply online for one (or more) of a company's JPA's. It is a no-win situation, and will be the only scenario presented to job seekers scrambling to become corporate employees. The game is designed to trap you into applying first, and then give you the illusion that you will have the opportunity to ask questions later. Only you will not be asking any questions about the company's EVP unless you are selected by a recruiter for further consideration. And even then, recruiters know that you will be too busy trying to get through the recruitment process instead of focusing on the company's lack of EVP transparency.

"Bank of America, trying to break free from a pile of bad mortgages and a sagging stock price, announced plans to lay off 30,000 employees over the next few years." – www.abcnews.go.com

The best workers are no longer willing to just accept a job at face value. Why should they when some of the best-known companies are laying off employees in droves? The internet and social media are at your disposal to learn about a company's EVP from current and former employees. It is up to you to use your social networks to quickly verify a company's claims before you apply, or make an employment decision. Do not let a recruiter or Hiring Manager simply sell only the good aspects of the JPA (and workplace environment) without questioning them about how the company is addressing the bad aspects. Companies have always expected and required that you be transparent during the application and interview process. They do not mince words when they state that any employment offer is contingent upon successful completion of a background check. For some reason, companies have not been held to the same standard by which they hold job seekers. The expectation is that you should just trust that a company is being truthful about its workplace environment and the duties listed on its JPA's. However, it will be you who will get fired – or have your career derailed – if you fail to clarify important details that can impact your ability to deliver sustained value.

"Cisco Systems Inc. has recently announced it would lay off 6,500 employees, or 9% of its full-time workforce. The company aims to trim about $1 billion from its operating costs. But some question whether this is enough, so this number could increase. Consequently, news outlets have claimed that as many as 10,000 layoffs will be announced." – www.huffingtonpost.com

Many companies embellish JPA's, CSC's, and the workplace environment in order to lure top job seekers to apply. Unfortunately, these companies are not held accountable for any major discrepancies of their implicit and implied selling statements. Even given this information disparity, you will be inclined to put a *"golden halo"* on your target employers because you have already been sprinkled with the fairy dust of employer branding campaigns. It will be difficult for you to separate the "real employer" from the "ideal employer" that is constantly sold to you throughout the corporate recruitment game. If you do not know what you want out of an employer, then any employer will do just fine. There are plenty of employers who are all-too-happy to sell you their special brand of snake oil (EBHP) so you will need to develop an independent judgment of your target companies. It will also behoove you to speak with any current employees not connected to the game: these will be the ones who are not Corporate Agents running around spewing corporate jargon in every other sentence they speak.

Many companies will publicly state what employees can expect from their workplace environments, but those expectations don't usually match up to the realities. For example, a company might say they value innovation and creativity; however, it's doubtful you'll be able to generate much of either if you're working 12-hour days in an understaffed department. **Companies will go to great lengths to hide the dirty details of their workplace environment and will practice a *"don't ask, don't tell"* policy: meaning if you do not ask the correct questions, they will not give you the correct answers.** The more transparent an employer brand, the higher the probability of discovering the actual conditions under which you will work, and whether those conditions are the best for your career. Nowadays, companies do more work to obscure the negative aspects of their EVP in hopes of getting your foot in the door first. They know that it will be much harder for you to voluntarily leave upon becoming an employee because of the high switching costs involved: relocation, income disruption, family obligations, etc. Companies attempt to uncover any negative aspects of your employee value proposition when they conduct a thorough background check and competency assessment. They don't just take what you say at face value: and why should they? You're not trying to convince a company to hire you based on your worst traits. The same holds true for your target companies: they are not trying to sell you on their worst traits. Therefore, shouldn't you thoroughly investigate their employer value proposition during your pre-employment phase activities?

"HSBC has been cutting jobs in countries including the United States and the United Kingdom, with plans to eliminate 30,000 jobs worldwide by the end of 2013." – www.huffingtonpost.com

Before employers advertise JPA's to the public, they have already decided which details of a job seeker's application will be the deal breakers that lead to an automatic rejection. This holds true for both job seekers following the rules of the formal recruitment process and those breaking the rules. However, it is unlikely that most job seekers have identified their own personal deal breakers that will prompt them to reject employers not meeting their standards. Very few companies would remain in business if they did not take stock of the deal breakers that could affect their operations and business goals. Carrefour, a French conglomerate, found this out the hard way. They planned to merge their Brazilian operations with Companhia Brasileira de Distribuição (owned by Grupo Pão de Açúcar: GPA) until it was revealed that one of Carrefour's competitors had a significant holding in GPA: thus, effectively derailing the merger plans. As you can imagine, this was a huge blow to Carrefour's expansion plans in one of the world's fastest growing markets. In order to avoid this fate when considering your employment options, you will need to know the deal breakers – both yours and the company's. Your target companies will not voluntarily disclose their EVP metrics in transparent detail, therefore, you will bear the onus of discovering the truth using your own methods – lest you end up dumbstruck like Carrefour.

Conclusion

"When you're prepared, you're more confident. When you have a strategy, you're more comfortable." – Fred Couples

Think of corporate recruiters and Hiring Managers as the bookends on a disturbingly inefficient and ineffective corporate recruitment process that you are expected to waste your valuable time pursuing. They are the major players in the corporate recruitment game you will battle against if you fall victim to employer branding mirages. Trying to get past one, and on to the other, involves a process that will keep you twisting and turning like a sea bass trapped in a fisherman's net. Your path to get a job with corporations through the formal recruitment process is littered with Venus Flytraps under the guise of: **1) career sites; 2) job postings; 3) applicant tracking systems; 4) psychometric tests; 5) interviews; 6) assessment centers; and 7) employment offers.** It is designed only for the so-called "best and brightest" to make it through the obstacle-course game, and onto the yellow brick road to speak with a recruiter. The corporate recruitment game is not known to the masses, and thus, it is they who disproportionately fall prey to its unwritten rules. Now that you have a realistic understanding of the game and how it is played to determine the outcome of your job search, don't get suckered into playing it.

When you apply online, you are left to the whims of the corporate recruiter to advance you in the process, and to the mercy of the Hiring Manager to decide if you will be extended an employment offer. The CSC's of most global employers will state that they value employees who are innovative, creative, and achievement-oriented. Employees who think outside the box, find alternative solutions to tough challenges, and show resiliency during tough times are often viewed (and treated) as exemplary employees to be tapped into the ranks of the corporate promotables. Ironically, these same companies have created a single-point of failure by designing a recruitment process that funnels all job seekers through the same online channel: the ATS, and its master, the corporate recruiter. When you are rejected by the recruiter, then you have to pack your bags, go home, and redo the entire "apply and wait" process with another company – or the same company, if indeed you are clinically insane. Remember, **it is not the corporate recruiter you are trying to work for, or who is the best person to judge your value to the Hiring Manager.** A recruiter will be able to properly judge your value only if he has functional experience from the business unit he supports. But that is a rarity you can only hope and pray to experience. Indeed, you'll have better luck "Finding Nemo" than finding a competent recruiter.

The real tragedy for job seekers is the continued use of a corporate recruitment game that conditions them to be singular-minded drones. How much "thinking outside the box" does it require to apply online and study the cookie-cutter interview questions that virtually all recruiters and Hiring Managers ask? Perhaps companies value the creative and innovative ways a job seeker can tweak a résumé to trick the Applicant Tracking System. Or perhaps they value the myriad interviewing strategies job seekers use to overcome the tough challenges of responding properly to telephone, video, and onsite interviews. Maybe these companies should add the following requirement on their JPA's: "*Ability to skillfully write a résumé and properly answer interview questions is highly desired.*" While it isn't realistic to avoid the corporate recruitment game altogether, job seekers can significantly reduce their dependency on it by focusing more of their time on the targeted job search. While this method is more time consuming, it is also more rewarding because you work from your own playbook instead of being played by a recruiter.

You will need to teach yourself some new tricks in order to emerge as a winner in the constantly changing employment landscape. Leave your old ways of job searching in the past. Even if those ways worked before, they can't be relied upon to provide the same results. The game changes much too rapidly for you to ever gain a sustained advantage. Challenge yourself to create and innovate, lest you wait and stagnate. Ralph Waldo Emerson said: "*A foolish consistency is the hobgoblin of little minds.*" It is indeed quite foolish to continue the same ineffective tactics while expecting different results. The new reality in the job market is that it is no longer blurred by national borders and restricted jobs. If you want the challenging jobs that will satisfy your career goals and allow you to grow and prosper professionally, then you will need to present yourself as a person of "value", and you will need to form strategic alliances within your social networks. These are the underpinnings of the targeted job search as well as the most effective alternative to playing the corporate recruitment game.

Using the targeted job search will allow you to leapfrog the marsh pit of the formal recruitment process, but there will still be obstacles to overcome in convincing the Hiring Manager of your value. It is the corporation that created the game so you will never truly be able to escape all of its pitfalls. By avoiding the obvious traps inherent in the formal recruitment process, you will at least even the odds of winning. However, Hiring Managers are an integral part of the corporate recruitment game, and will oftentimes resist being used as a pawn in your backdoor operation to circumvent the formal recruitment process. Therefore, you will have to work smart to convince them that it is worth their time to meet with you versus sending you kicking and screaming to the Human Resources department. **Your main task will be to unplug Hiring Managers from the corporate recruitment game so that they are able to recognize you as an asset – not an applicant.** Find their Achilles Heel (business pain points) and you might just get the opening you need to win over the most powerful player in the game.

Do not be in such a rush to get hired that you forget to thoroughly research your target companies. Misjudging an employer can come with a high cost to your career brand in both present and future professional opportunities. There have been, and will continue to be, job seekers whose careers are derailed because they blindly accepted a supposedly good job offer, only to find out later that it was the worst decision for their career track. Examples and real life stories are not hard to come by. One recent quote on Glassdoor.com from an employee working at HSBC – who obviously misjudged its employer brand – states, *"Where careers come to die. People are not considered a competitive advantage. Little to no investment in undergraduates, training opportunities, etc. Very individualistic – most are not team players. Extremely hierarchal. Tendency to rest on their name and people are not made accountable. The management of expenses is horrendous and careless."* That statement provides a stark contrast to the employer brand that most major corporations attempt to sell. How much value do you think that employee is adding to his career brand each day he works for an employer he obviously believes has oversold, and under delivered on its employer brand promise?

It is ironic how a company can value transparency in aspects of its business that are legally mandated by the government and financial agencies; but not in the aspects of its recruitment, hiring, and employer branding. Transparency is anathema to the corporate recruitment game, and full disclosure will affect a company's ability to attract and retain the best workers. Finding a company with an employer branding campaign that actually matches its employer value proposition will not be easy. It would be ideal if global companies produced detailed reports of their EVP equivalent to their Annual Reports and Sustainability Reports. That would give you an official document to compare against other employers, and allow you to choose which ones to pursue based on their alignment with your professional objectives. But don't wait on companies to deliver that gift horse! In today's competitive business climate, the corporate recruitment game is in overdrive: companies seek to gain a competitive advantage by hiring the top university graduates and professionals on the one hand, and by hoarding talent to the detriment of their competitors on the other.

The global companies who play the corporate recruitment game will make metrics-based decisions when selecting, evaluating, and hiring. They will commit very few mistakes: therefore, you will not have many openings to enter through their pearly gates. Most job seekers will never get past the ATS, but recruiters have already discounted them as collateral damage. There will be no tears shed for the job applicants who put all their hopes and dreams into working for their target employers, but fail to meet the parameters of the standard corporate employee mold. Corporate recruiters are safari hunting for big game only – not field mice. The big game recruits are the employee equivalents of entrepreneurs like Mark Zuckerberg and Sergey Brin: talented individuals who can create extraordinary corporate wealth. If you don't want to be a pawn in the corporate recruitment game, you will need to have your career objectives and target companies mapped out before deciding your job search strategy. If you have the profile that fits the corporate employee mold, then applying online might be a gamble worth taking under the right circumstances. However, it would be unwise to rely solely on that method when it is filled with so many briar patches and thorn bushes that could snag even the most talented of job seekers. In the corporate recruitment game, you will be played no matter what move you make: whether you decide to play or not, is up to you.

The Job Seekers' Fables

"Beware the Jabberwock, my son! The jaws that bite, the claws that catch! Beware the Jubjub bird, and shun the frumious Bandersnatch!" – Lewis Carroll

There is no better way to tell a story than through fables that teach a valuable lesson. I wrote the Job Seekers' Fables to illustrate how different individuals approach the corporate recruitment game. Just like the fable of *"The Three Little Pigs"*, many individuals construct their job search out of straw, sticks, or bricks – with the same equivalent results! Nowadays, job seekers fit the mold of baby birds, vultures, or eagles.

The Baby Birds

Job seekers have become dependent on what I call the *"baby bird"* syndrome. This is where the mother bird flies from the nest each day to go find worms and bugs to bring back to the nest to feed the little baby bird hatchlings. Those little birds become dependent on the mother bird until she kicks them out of the nest. And then for the first time in their lives, they actually have to compete for food in the open market. And there are plenty of predators in the open market! JPA's lull these job seekers to sleep and into a helpless trance of "apply and wait" just like baby birds in a nest. These job seekers have forgotten how (or don't see the value in) to network for success. The term, networking, is so overused now that the very word has lost some of its efficacy. But in fact it has always been the key to employment – even in ancient times! Word of mouth is how many people differentiated themselves, their handy crafts, their services, their labor, etc. But somewhere along the way, along with all the advances in technology, people forgot to spend more time talking (and listening!) to other people, and began to rely on sending job applications into cyberspace. Technology has made people dependent on JPA's just like the little baby birds are dependent on the mother bird for food. Do you really want to be the job seeker who sits around in misery because companies are not posting the jobs that YOU want, nor responding favorably when you apply?

The Vultures

These job seekers are the most frightening of all! They are the first to apply to any new JPA in cyberspace. They will hover around the same job boards and career sites, and will apply to the same companies over and over and over. They don't just apply and wait: they apply and hover over a JPA until it withers away and dies. Long after the job has been filled, they will continue to harass the company in hopes of getting lucky. They are well-known in cyberspace, and already have multiple warrants out for their capture and dismissal from the applicant tracking system. They are the "me too" job seekers who have nothing of value to offer a company. They will pounce on any company's job board and will use résumé blasting services to reach thousands of employers. They don't even remember (or care) who they apply to. They just want a job – and any job will do! They can no longer discern a good JPA from a bad JPA. They wake up each morning like mindless zombies on a singular mission: find new job postings! Indeed, after their long search, and feasting on the carcasses of long discarded job postings, they will eventually get hired. And they will bring great misery and heartache to the poor company that does hire them! These job seekers specialize in finding companies with poor selection and interviewing processes. Do you really want to conduct a job search where only the most desperate (or foolish) companies will hire you?

The Eagles

These are the job seekers who could care less about JPA's. In fact, they rarely use job boards and career sites to conduct their search. They are soaring high in the sky, and always looking out for opportunities and new challenges. They have excellent vision and can see possibilities where others see doubt. They operate with precision and accuracy, and do not waste their energy on foolish endeavors. They are fierce competitors and do not easily give up at the first sign of difficulty. They have confidence and skills that attract employers to them. They are the objects of a company's desire: top employers will go to great lengths to find them. They are in the best position to negotiate the type of job they want as well as the compensation package they are worth. These job seekers are also job creators who can work for themselves. If they don't see something that appeals to them, they will study the market and find a niche that they can build into a company. They seek to leverage their strengths to present a value proposition to prospective employers, clients, and customers. They are highly evolved, and sit at the apex of the job seekers' food chain. They are few in number, and never have to worry about the competing job seekers at the bottom of the pyramid. They usually become the future Aliko Dangote, Steve Jobs, Lakshmi Mittal, Sergey Brin, Mark Zuckerberg, Carlos Slim, and other exceptional entrepreneurs in the world. Companies can only hope that they will become the next high-potential job seekers to enter the corporate recruitment game.

Outro

"The number of those who undergo the fatigue of judging for themselves is very small indeed." – Richard Brinsley Sheridan

I hope you enjoyed reading "The Corporate Recruitment Game" as much as I enjoyed writing it. I hope that I was able to connect with you on some level, and provide you with a unique insight into the corporate recruitment process and all of its connected parts. Even though the pages of this book are sprinkled with humor, it is not meant to detract from the seriousness of the matter at hand. There are scores of newly unemployed people every day, and many of them are struggling to find jobs that provide a living wage along with decent working conditions. There are also scores of newly graduated college students who have yet to find a job but are not counted as being unemployed by any of the official jobless statistics. Many of these people could benefit from understanding how the corporate recruitment game operates. Instead of wasting their time chasing the pipe dream of being a highly-paid corporate employee, they can redirect their efforts into becoming an economically independent entrepreneur. What many people don't realize is that it takes roughly the same effort and energy to try and work for someone else as it does to work for yourself.

Since so many college-educated job seekers are focused on becoming employees, they oftentimes forget to consider how they can use their ksa's to earn money for themselves. This doesn't have to be a long-term solution for job seekers, but it is definitely an entrepreneurial activity that will keep their spirits high and their skills sharp while they continue their job search campaign. Some might just get lucky and stumble upon an entrepreneurial passion they didn't know existed. The possibilities are endless, but only if you take that first step of doing an economic activity instead of relying solely on an application activity. While writing this book, I was constantly thinking of who I thought would most benefit from reading it. My objective is not to discourage people from becoming corporate employees; it is to encourage people to not sit idly by and let someone else decide their employment prospects. I want people to take control of their career management and learn how to survive this new era of corporate employment that will leave more losers than winners. My target audience can be broken down into the following four segmentations:

1. **High School Students.** If your school has a Career Academy or Vocational Program, I implore you to take advantage of them. Why? Because these courses will allow you to develop the basic skills necessary to do either of the following: 1) enter the workforce immediately; 2) enter college with a defined career objective; 3) start your own business. Have frequent conversations with your school's career counselor and ask her for advice on how you can get professional experience and exposure to your career-related interests. Don't be afraid to choose your own path after high school as opposed to following a path chosen by someone else. Learning is a lifelong endeavor that will consist of both formal and informal education.

2. **College Students.** Identify the students who are smart and entrepreneurial. These will be the ones you need to stick close to. Participate in as many business plan competitions and company-sponsored case challenges related to your interests as possible. Work as many internships (paid or unpaid) with your target companies as possible in order to add the maximum value to your professional brand. Don't graduate college without having started your own business – no matter how small it is. The skills you will learn from launching your own enterprise will set you apart from the average student: and may also allow you to stumble upon a long-term venture.

3. **College Graduates.** The interests of global corporations and the interests of global universities are completely misaligned. Just graduating with a degree is no longer a guarantee for a good paying job. Companies are not just interested in your formal degree; they are interested in what you can do to give

them a competitive advantage. Universities are more concerned with preparing you to be a well-rounded employee rather than an opportunity-spotting entrepreneur. If you are unable to effectively sell yourself to a company recruiter, then you will find yourself bogged down in a long and frustrating job search.

4. **Experienced Professionals.** Take the time to establish how your ksa's add to your company's bottom line and be sure to keep those skills updated. Establish a robust professional network that is able to introduce you directly to Hiring Managers at your target companies. Study the latest job search and career management strategies even when you are not in the job market. If you are a corporate drone, then be on the lookout for any indications that you or your department will be affected by layoffs. If you are a corporate promotable, then beware if your career stalls, as that might not bode well for your continued employment. Develop a risk management strategy that will provide short-term security should you find yourself unexpectedly unemployed. Otherwise, you might be tempted to get sucked into a corporate recruitment game for which you'll be ill-prepared to play.

About The Author

"I pass, like night, from land to land; I have strange power of speech; that moment that his face I see, I know the man that must hear me: To him my tale I teach." – Samuel T. Coleridge

Roderick Emanuel Lewis is a pioneering researcher, writer, and Thought Leader in Analytical Workplace Metrics, which evaluates the workplace environment by applying objective data critical to maximizing the employee-employer relationship. With a focus on the corporate recruitment process, he has developed career assessment objectives for job seekers as well as talent acquisition and branding strategies for employers.

Roderick's work is informed by personal experiences as job seeker and entrepreneur along with professional expertise honed in the corporate workplace and in the academic arena – as teacher, consultant, and designer of career and international recruitment programs. He is fluent in Spanish and Portuguese; years of residency and graduate-level teaching in both countries have framed his interests in global marketing, diversity and inclusion issues, and social media networking.

Born and raised in Tuscaloosa, Alabama, Roderick earned a Bachelor's degree in Electrical Engineering from the University of Alabama. After he worked a few years as a Process Controls Engineer, a growing interest in international business led him to the Georgia Institute of Technology's MBA program; while matriculating, he studied abroad in Costa Rica, Mexico, and Spain, immersing himself in Spanish language and culture. More international travel followed his MBA degree and cemented his professional pursuits

Roderick is an avid writer and regular contributor to *Top MBA Quarterly* and *Universum Quarterly*, the world's leading employer branding journal. He currently resides in Lisbon, Portugal, where he directs the International Relations program for a university's business school.

Connect with the Author –
Email: lewisrod@gmail.com
LinkedIn: http://www.linkedin.com/in/lewisrod
Webinar: http://youtu.be/Ekn5XrM4fKl
Op-Ed articles: http://www.scribd.com/voiceofthejobseeker

www.ingramcontent.com/pod-product-compliance
Lightning Source LLC
Chambersburg PA
CBHW020741180526
45163CB00001B/307